7-19-

CHILDREN OF THE BLITZ

MEMORIES OF WARTIME CHILDHOOD

COMPILED BY ROBERT WESTALL

VIKING

For John Geer, a Child of the Blitz

VIKING

Penguin Books Ltd, Harmondsworth, Middlesex, England
Viking Penguin Inc., 40 West 23rd Street, New York, New York 10010, U.S.A.
Penguin Books Australia Ltd, Ringwood, Victoria, Australia
Penguin Books Canada Ltd, 2801 John Street, Markham, Ontario, Canada
L3R 1B4
Penguin Books (N.Z.) Ltd, 182–190 Wairau Road, Auckland 10, New Zealand

First published 1985

Typeset in Monophoto Photina with Univers display

Printed in Great Britain by Butler & Tanner Ltd, Frome and London

Designed by Peter Ward

Library of Congress Catalog Card Number: 85–51165

British Library Cataloguing in Publication Data

Westall, Robert
    The children of the Blitz: memories of wartime childhood.
    1. World War, 1939–1945—Children—Great Britain   2. Children—Great
    Britain—History—20th century   3. Great Britain—Social life and customs—
    20th century
    I. Title
941.084′088054   D810.C4

ISBN 0–670–80134–8

Contents

Contributors

At the risk of seeming invidious, I must single out some people; because they contributed not just incidents, but whole ways of life.

First 'Boy, London' – the incomparable John Geer, to whom this book is dedicated; crawling down a foot-wide tunnel to damp down a phosphorus bomb at the age of fourteen; crawling under collapsed houses to separate the living from the dead at the age of seventeen – 'because I was the smallest'. Whenever I read in *The Times* that some notable 'had a good war' I think of John Geer.

'Girl, London', his doughty six-year-old counterpart, was Jean Underhill. I'm glad girls figure largely. Bessie Shea was my Orkney correspondent, who opened my eyes to a much livelier 'Phoney War' than most of us knew, round the British naval base of Scapa Flow. A mixture of Heinkel seaplanes and Sunday School outings; dead men washed ashore, salvaged kegs of butter and Bible classes.

Then there was my adorable communist grammar-school evacuee, Doreen Manwaring, battering away at the English class system in Folkestone, and hoping that the German bomber overhead will get away; though I couldn't resist showing her change of attitude as a Cambridge student, once Russia had entered the war. And lastly, A.C. Wilson, actually under the Nazi jackboot in Holland.

The boys, though, were after adventure. 'Boy, Tyneside', in hot pursuit of bowler-hatted spies and German POWs was Aidan Harrison. Leading the real-life 'machine-gunners' of Withernsea was Reg Tomes. Cycling round blitzed Coventry with a bomb on his crossbar was Len Nugent, now of Barrack Heights, New South Wales. Michael Hyde collected his arsenal of weapons in Northamptonshire; John Houghton was the armigerous 'Boy, Edinburgh'.

And there were gentler souls. Alex Hastie in Northumberland discovered his abiding 'love of country life'. The thoughtful 'Boy, Manchester' was Keith Mottram. I'll leave you to guess who the other 'Boy, Tyneside' was . . .

Otherwise, I'd like to thank, for their memories:
S. Balmforth; Emma Bell; R. Bennet; B.E. Bleckley; C. Board; J.M. Bowen; Chris Brazier; Lillian Cheeseman; Alan Campbell Cooke;

H.S. Cousins; Alan Cross; Mary Davies; Janet Diamond; Miss I. Drennan; Betty Dutton; Paddy Easton; Richard Elliot; Ronnie Gaffery; Sarah Goodman; T. Gordon; Joan Henry; Irene Hosking; H. Jones; J. Jones; Mrs Lamb; Colin Lynch; G.J. McEntaggart; Mrs McEntaggart; Mr Morison; S. Peake; A.E. Prior; Rosemary Ralph; M.A. Read; Hazel Reddy; Mr Ringstead; M. Roberts; Mrs Robertson; Jill Rodwell; Peter Rutter; Richard Eyan; George Saven; Margaret Smith; N. Stead; Mr Stead; S. Thomas; Michael Towey; John Charles West; A. Williams; C. Winrow; P. Woolley; Mrs E. Woolley.

Next I must thank Mrs Caroline Aherne, Deputy Head of Ellesmere Port Catholic High School, and her intrepid team of young researchers who opened up for me 'the war on Merseyside'. Their names are: S. Balmforth; Kay Colligan; Debby Cook; Aidan Daly; Catharine Ellison; Tracey Fielding; P. Harris; Martha Jones; Robert Keir; M. McEntaggart; Sandra Morison; Colin Murphy; Michael Omar; Angela Pacetta; William Peake; Christopher Reddy; Rachel Reed; Joanne Ringstead; Andrew Roberts; Emma Robertson; Kerry Ryan; Andrew L. Simcott; Carol Smyth; Karen Swarbrick; Delia Sworm; Anthony Thompson; Gerard Tran; John A. West; Gordon Wilson; Michelle Winrow; Stephen J. Woolley.

Lastly, I must thank the Imperial War Museum's Department of Printed Records, and especially Ms Valerie France, and the Librarian of the Royal Marines' Regimental Museum, Portsmouth.

Robert Westall

'Of those who stayed put with their parents, a few were continuously nervous, and a few constantly exhilarated. The greater part adjusted as well as their parents or mildly better. At no stage did they present a special problem as compared, for example, with old ladies, or stray pets.'

Tom Harrison (Mass Observation), *Living through the Blitz*

'I would rather be bombed to fragments than leave England.'

Boy's letter to the press

'It's just as dangerous here as in Southampton. Now I can get my own souvenirs.'

Boy evacuee (Dorset) rejoicing in watching air battles

'The reader will not credit that such things could be, but I was there and I saw it.'

Izaak Walton

Introduction   I didn't find the Children of the Blitz; they found me. It began when I wrote *The Machine-gunners* in 1975; a book about kids in the Second World War who find a crashed German bomber, steal its machine-gun and set out to fight their own war against the Germans. *The Times* mistakenly reviewed it as adult fiction, calling it 'Just William – with tears'. But next day the critic's wife wrote to me, saying how much it had brought back memories of cowering in the shelter during the Portsmouth Blitz.

She was only the first. More than half the letters I received in the following months were from forty-year-olds, wanting to share their war with me: people like Len Nugent, writing from Barrack Heights, New South Wales, with a hair-raising tale of cycling round blitzed Coventry with an unexploded bomb tied to his crossbar. As the heap of letters grew, it became clear there had been more than one 'secret war'. For the things the kids got up to, all questionable, many illegal, and some downright lethal, would have sent their parents into fits – if the parents hadn't been too busy, too worried, too tired to notice.

There was a whole Children's War, never recorded. What was more, by the mid-1970s the Children of the Blitz were already dying off. When the real-life 'Machine-gunners' finally surfaced in 1979 (in the form of the late church choir of Withernsea, Humberside), indignant to know how I had learnt their secret, two of them had already died in their fifties. If a history of the Children's War was not going to be lost for ever, it was now or never.

Research was a nightmare. How do you reach material locked in the memories of five million self-effacing people, many of whom found even setting pen to paper a massive act of courage? In the end, I simply asked everyone I met who seemed to be the right age. At first they would say 'No, nothing out of the ordinary ever happened to me.' Then a glint of memory would come into their eye ... hints and snatches, like the female colleague who said: 'The German POWs took me rabbit-shooting in the Pennines when I was five. I fell into a gorse-bush and they picked me up and pulled all the prickles out of me, and carried me straight home to my mother, ruining their day.' But she wouldn't write an account of it ...

I know this book has only scratched the surface; my research was no more than a hurried, scattered rescue-dig. I know that far more hair-raising and incredible stories wait to be uncovered. Perhaps they will now come pouring in.

The word 'incredible' falls like a knell. I know this book is not history, not *pukka* history. Tom Harrison of Mass Observation, working during the Blitz itself, found that people's eye-witness accounts at the time of being bombed varied very greatly from accounts rendered only three months later. And I am working forty years later ... forty years for people to hone and polish their stories, to present themselves in a more heroic light. My collection is what was called in my wife's family 'grandad stories'. Some very dubious stuff certainly came in, like this: 'My primary teacher told us that he was a boy in the war. He and a friend were passing this big mansion that had been left empty when people went to the war and they saw this curtain twitch and they thought it might be a spy so they told the police and they went and caught the spy ...' That story tells more about the primary teacher than German spies, however incompetent some of them were.

Most of the stories were not so self-aggrandizing – but inconsequential, comical, self-mocking. Nevertheless, I had to rely on my ear as a writer, that knows the salt, wry sound of reality; and the memory of the ten-year-old Blitz kid I was, who knew the sinking in the gut at the sound of the siren, the smell of cordite on the autumn air, the taste of dried egg and spam. So I have made my selection of war-myths composed, as Wordsworth would have said, of emotion recollected over forty years of tranquillity. What else is *any* autobiography?

Compiling this book has been humbling. I now know my own war, on which I based *The Machine-gunners*, was a very unexciting war which, in the safe North of England, went away in the spring of 1942 and never came back. I desperately wanted to reach fifteen, and be messenger to my Dad, who was an ARP sector-leader with the wardens. But by the time I reached fifteen, all the wardens were doing was running whist drives. My war after spring 1942 was made up of passing for grammar school, American swing records, girls and trying to get in the school rugby team. The war had faded to a matter of newspapers and newsreels.

What the Children of the Blitz have shown me is that they found the war *fun*; the best game anybody ever invented, unless you or somebody near and dear got killed. Even Bernard Kops, in the hell of the East End 1940 bombing, found new and exciting toys in the slot-machines of the Underground. Children take and make their fun where they can get it, and if it's potentially lethal, that just makes it *more* fun. Nobody ever played cowboys-and-Indians like the three heroes of Barmouth, with real stolen rifles, real ammunition, and real British commandos to shoot at. They had learnt the game of war only too well. Thank God they also knew about the white flag of surrender; perhaps first heard of at the Fall of Singapore . . .

And if the pacifists don't like this fact, they're going to have to lump it.

What struck me most was the childlike directness of the writing; it seemed almost as if we forty- and fifty-year-olds had shed our grey hairs and wrinkled hides and reverted to the Children of the Blitz we were. That was my idea in making this book – a history of children, by children, for children . . . an attempt to counteract the endless poison of the war-comics, that get more violent, more xenophobic, more distanced from common humanity every year.

You don't get Nazis carrying a little girl home to her mother, at the expense of ruining their day, in war-comics. I wonder what today's children will make of it.

WE SELL
Sphere
SUSPENDERS
WE SELL
Sphere
A.R.P. OUTFITS
FUR
RESTORATION
New Beautifying Process.

CHAPTER 1 LAST DAYS OF PEACE

26 AUGUST 1939 THE LAST NIGHT OF PEACE

I'm dressed up in my Sunday best – tweed belted overcoat the exact replica of my father's; shorts coming just below the knee; shoes my mother's polished till they shine like coal; and the schoolboy cap that's never off my head because it's so useful. For catching butterflies, carrying shells home from the beach, fanning our fire, cleaning blackboards for teacher and above all, fighting in the schoolyard. Folded, with the hard brim outwards, it's a formidable weapon.

I feel different inside when I put on Sunday best. I expect to feel uncomfortable, know I mustn't run, play tag, climb walls. Once, I put my shoes on the wrong feet and never noticed till I got home, because feeling cramped is part of feeling grand, going round the town.

We never set off till dusk, however late that is. Going round the town doesn't work in daylight. It can't start till the lamp-lighter, strange silent man whistling under his breath, never talking to us boys because he's in too much of a hurry, has put his ladder against the iron arms of the lampposts and lit them.

Round the town is a gaslit world. Naked gas-jets flaring inside all the shops and outside, too, at the shopkeeper's expense. Gas-jets flaring in the pork-butcher's, against the huge mirrors that cloud and clear as the great clouds of cooking-steam hit them. So that at one moment my face, peering in the pork-butcher's window, stares back at me; and next moment it's just a misty blur, creepy as a ghost, so I only know it's me because when I raise an arm it waves back.

15

The smell of boiling pork, from the seething bath-size cauldrons, drifts down Saville Street like a hymn in some great cathedral. The pork-shop woman (immensely fat from sampling her own cooking when her back's turned and she thinks no one can see) drips sweat from her pale cheeks and nose as if she was being cooked herself, the biggest pig of all. The whole pigs hanging from sharp steel hooks in the ceiling look slim by comparison. Their skins are scraped as smooth and white as film stars. I reach out and touch one; the skin is horribly like my own, but colder than I ever get, even in winter. I try poking my hand into the long narrow slit where the pig's life once was, and catch the woman watching me in the misted mirror. I pretend to scuff my diamond-bright shoes instead, making half-moons of bare scrubbed planking in the thick sawdust of the floor.

But she's too busy to put a hand across my face (which we both know she's perfectly entitled to do, and my father would clout me as well, if he saw her do it). Too busy in her frantic Saturday night orgy of feeding ten thousand hungry faces coming in for penny-dips (just a bun dipped in the seething cauldron till it's red-hot) or a saveloy-dip (containing a curiously wrinkled sausage), or best of all a fourpenny pork-sandwich with stuffing. Each is wrapped in a sheet of white paper, dropped as soon as the customer has finished eating it outside. The blizzard of white paper spreads out and out from the pork-shop as the night goes on, like an early White Christmas. There's no other litter, except the great piles of horse-droppings that are spread wider and wider by passing cartwheels, until they're as big and thin as hearth-rugs.

But the crossing-sweepers are already busy, will be working past midnight, for the streets must be spotless for folks going to church tomorrow morning.

Everybody walks and stands in the cobbled street. The only cars belong to rich folk, and are safely away in the garage. There's a few steam-lorries parked in side-streets, black and gently hissing, with tall chimneys and boilers you can warm your hands against.

Sometimes when you're standing talking, you feel a nudge on your shoulder, and there's a dark-eyed blinkered horse with a lamp-flickering cart behind, waiting to get past.

No room on the pavements. The shop awnings are out, in case it rains, and from them hang chains of two-shilling boots and shoes, ranks of boilersuits and dungarees, and the sad dark overcoats that poor people buy, looking drooping and defeated even before they've begun to fight. (We, grander, buy ours at the Fifty-Shilling Tailors.)

More cheerful are the fruit sellers with their covered barrows and flaring acetylene glowing over a landscape of oranges, apples and tomatoes, penny a pound.

We push through in single file, father leading. His head never stops nodding. 'Now, George? ... What fettle the day, Harry? ... Hallo, Nick, how's the missus?' Occasionally he turns back to my mother.

'See who that was?'

'No,' says my Mam, eyes on some real silk stockings for elevenpence three-farthings.

'Little Nesser – served me time wi' him at the North-eastern.'

'Oh, aye,' says Mam, eyes returning to the silk stockings, her lips moving in silent computation.

Music, every few yards. A man with no legs, sitting on a doorstep, playing a mouth-organ, his cap on the pavement beside him, guarded by a small white fox terrier. I stare at where his

On the brink: we were already carrying gasmasks, but on Saturday night the shop windows were still ablaze with light, and the shops were open till nine, as they were never to be again.

legs should be; great fat pads of black leather instead. He seems quite happy playing there among a forest of legs. At least he has no legs to stick out and trip up passers-by.

My usual creepy curiosity overcomes me; to dare get close to him. I ask Dad for a ha'penny to put in his cap; one of my Saturday night privileges. I get it; am mistakenly praised for my soft heart. I run up to him in a flurry, stealing tiny glances at his face, which is fat, lined, very alive. As my ha'penny clinks down, he glances up and I flee before he can say anything. If I let him speak, I'd have to admit that he's human. I'd rather think of him as a fabulous beast, like the Headless Woman at the fairground . . .

A woman plays an accordion, very loud and dramatic, eyes fixed on the chimney-pots across the road. Is she mad, or merely blind?

More cheerful, a huge man and his very small wife sing a duet. 'Roses are flowering in Picardy . . .' If you creep very close, you can hear him mutter to her, with every intake of breath, 'Sing up, you bugger.'

Then we meet somebody we *really* know. George Lee, sea-cook, fresh off his ship, a little capuchin monkey on his shoulder, shivering in a red flannel jacket and helping itself feverishly to peanuts from his breast-pocket, cracking them with expert black-leather fingers. The monkey and I stare at each other. It seems much older than me, wiser. Does it know all about Hitler? It sums me up as being of no account, and goes back to frantic nutcracking.

Now we really are stuck for an hour. George will take my father on his latest tour of the world, places like Gib, Rio, and Abadan, which sounds like Aberdeen but is in the Gulf . . . We could be stuck all night.

'Can I have me pocket-money?' My father reaches into his pocket, without stopping listening to how Musso's cleaned up the red-light district of Genoa. I have a vision of the great Italian dictator going round with one of Mam's dusters, polishing all the red traffic-lights of Italy. My father's hand comes down blindly – in a minute I shall know whether I'm merely rich, or very rich. Depends how much overtime he's worked; or how long he intends standing talking to George Lee.

Shilling! Great! Now I can stand for ages, staring through the window of Swan's toyshop, wondering whether to buy a model of a Fairey Battle bomber, or a Glasgow Corporation Tram, or save it towards the Royal Tank Corps light-tank set. Or go to the ends of the streets leading to the river and the great silent ships. There's an invisible chalk line drawn across those streets, which it is forbidden, if not downright fatal, for me to cross. Foreign sailors down there, and Women, and worst of all, the Maltese who run the Women. Sailors get stabbed to death every Saturday night, their wallets get lifted, and their bodies dropped into the river on the outgoing tide and never seen again.

But there's never anything to see, except big policemen in their pointed helmets, walking always in pairs under the distant gas-lamps.

'Don't get lost!' says Dad, now deep in discussion of a mummified mermaid George was offered for a quid in Djibouti, and now he could kick himself he didn't buy it for the kids.

I'm off on me own. There's dangers – the rows of slum-kids sitting on the doorsteps of the pubs, waiting for their monstrous parents to emerge in one or two or three hours' time. They'd twist my arm, have my pocket-money off me, if I was fool enough to go too near. Kids whose parents drink don't know no laws ... but they daren't move off their doorsteps, or their drunken sires would take their belt-buckle to them.

But the most gorgeous danger is Happy Ralph; a monster famous all over Tyneside, a gaunt figure in a bowler hat who lurks round the corner in Borough Road and will rush out at *anybody* with huge outstretched hands and strange cries. Whether to embrace people or strangle them will never be known, because no one hangs around long enough to find out. On Sundays, drawn by the hymn-singing, he goes into churches and menaces the quivering rows of spinsters in the pews, or even the vicar in his pulpit, bringing whole services to a standstill and being quite impossible to get rid of. It is one of our games in the school playground to shout 'Happy Ralph' and rush wildly at the girls, who scatter screaming.

Another strange beast roaming the dark is Knocker Loaftins, who makes a living selling sawdust to butchers. They promise him sixpence, if he'll carry it down the cellar; then only give him threepence. Whereupon Knocker picks up his bag again, and departs into the night with wild and incoherent screams.

Or there's the man who worked for years for the night-soil gang, emptying earth-closets, and as a result is said to have half his face eaten away by some foul disease.

In half an hour, I'm back. To find the monkey gone, replaced by my cousin Ada. Dad has just fatally asked Ada how her Mam is. Ada will now spend an hour giving us every symptom of every member of her family since we last saw her, which is at least a year, thank God.

Off to the little narrow tobacconist that sells hot sarsaparilla by the glass. You drink it sitting in his narrow mahogany booths,

CHURCHMAN'S CIGARETTES

A GARDEN DUG-OUT

CHURCHMAN'S CIGARETTES

EQUIPPING YOUR REFUGE ROOM—B

CHURCHMAN'S CIGARETTES

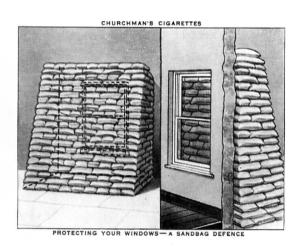

PROTECTING YOUR WINDOWS—A SANDBAG DEFENCE

CHURCHMAN'S CIGARETTES

EXTINCTION OF INCENDIARY BOMB

CHURCHMAN'S CIGARETTES

MEDIUM TRAILER FIRE-PUMP IN ACTION

CHURCHMAN'S CIGARETTES

A CHAIN OF BUCKETS

20

with prickly worn-leather seats, looking at the bits of your face showing up in his mirrors, cut into fragments by painted adverts for Gold Flake and Capstan Navy Cut. Great talker, this tobacconist, with his bald head, gold spectacles and long brown coat. He calls me 'my little man' and asks my opinion of the Polish Corridor and the latest Torso Murder Case. I have to hold my end up, because he knows my father, and tells him all the quaint and amusing replies I make ...

It's all dead safe *really*. Because everyone knows my father, or at least my Nana, and has seen me in my pram when I was two weeks old and knew my Auntie Rosie when she was a girl in the Last War and went on route-marches with the soldiers and carried their rifles when they got tired ...

The town is filling up now, you can hardly move. The cinemas must be out, the Rex, Albion, Princes, Boro', Howard Hall, Comedy and Carlton. The pubs, too, because there's Granda', grand in waistcoat watch, and gold Albert. He carries his skinful magnificently, only has a slight tendency to sing, which Nana stamps on firmly. The only other way I know is when I'm made to kiss him (which he hates as well) and I get a mouthful of whiskery sandpaper skin and a smell like a brewery. Honestly, if you held a match to his mouth he could blow out six-foot flames like a fire-eater ... Then he gives me a whole half-crown, which is final proof of total intoxication and is reduced to sixpence by the combined efforts of the whole family.

And so to bed.

But not to sleep.

I can't sleep because there's a torch and three large toy pistols under my pillow and they keep working down under my shoulders.

Is there going to be a war? That's why the torch and pistols are there. I think about the Germans; the situation is perfectly simple.

The Germans are the bullies of the European classroom. Lots of little countries have been getting their arms twisted behind their backs. But in the corner of that classroom, Britain is sitting, best fighter in the school, captain of football, popular hero. Britain has got her feet up on the windowsill at present, reading a book, because the bully hasn't gone too far. Yet! But when the little kids squeal too loud, Britain will get up and give the bully a bloody nose. The bully will crumple up, snivelling snots in the corner, and then we'll have peace.

Simple. Happened before, in 1918. Look at the map; half the world is coloured red, for British. Germany is a pathetic little green postage stamp; there is hardly room to print the word 'Berlin'.

I have one or two doubts. My father says the Germans are good engineers; he will buy me German toys; the rest are 'foreign rubbish'. My father respects German gunnery, after the Battle of Jutland, in the Last Lot. German captains keep clean ships; when they are in port, all their sailors march to the Seamen's Mission to worship in immaculate uniforms. The Germans, unlike the Latin races, are 'clean-living men'.

My mother is mortally afraid the U-boats will starve Britain to death. In the Last Lot she queued up four hours for a piece of suet, but when she got to the front of the queue, it had all gone. But U-boats are just another example of sneaky German cowardice, attacking unarmed merchant ships; when our destroyers get there, they always depth-charge them into soup!

German bombers have evil names like Dornier and Heinkel and Stuka. They have evil shapes, long, thin and pointed, like snakes and dragons, praying mantises and sting-rays. They are always painted black and carry the crooked cross. They only bomb women and children.

British planes are honest brown and green, and look like faithful dogs, with friendly names like Hurricane and Wellington and Hampden.

Suddenly I am stricken with doubts. Will our faithful dogs be able to cope with the poisonous dragons? Then I remember about the Supermarine Spitfire. I don't know anything about the Spitfire; I've only seen it on a cigarette card, and the artist didn't know much about the Spitfire either, because he's painted it coming out of the sun, with no details. But that Spitfire is black too, and looks even more shark-like and poisonous than the Germans.

Reassured, I remember about 'ersatz'. Everything the Germans have is 'ersatz'. They make 'ersatz' coffee by stealing acorns off their pigs and roasting them, and it tastes yuk, but they can't afford real coffee. Their soldiers' boots have ersatz cardboard soles that fall apart as soon as it rains. They're trying to make petrol out of potatoes because they haven't got any oil. (That's why they still pull their field-guns with horses.) All the oil and tin and rubber in the world comes from Malaya, which is part of the great British Empire. If a war comes, our Navy will starve them out. Like in the Last Lot.

And the Germans have the hopeless burden of Hitler – a total nutter, worse than Happy Ralph. If he can't get his own way, he falls down foaming at the mouth and chews the carpet. Every kid you meet is pulling a lock of hair down over his forehead, sticking his finger under his nose and screaming

We saw a lot of footage of Hitler at mass rallies on the newsreels. We laughed at his contortions and gibberings as we laughed at films of witchdoctors or Zulus dancing. The mass rallies were meant to be terrifying, but they made the Germans look like brainless sheep. And when they marched, their goose-step was a proper scream. *This unfailingly comical view of the Germans persisted until 1945, when we saw the newsreels of Buchenwald.*

fake German till his throat conks out or somebody kicks him. We do the goose-step till we fall over laughing. And there are songs . . .

> Ven der Führer says
> Ve iss der Master Race,
> Ve vart, vart,
> Right in der Führer's face . . .

Too many bravissimo performances of this epic have greatly increased our mothers' burden of underpants washing. Then that other song, to the tune of Colonel Bogie,

> Adolf . . . has only got one ball
> Goering . . . he has none at all . . .

(We would be enthralled, in 1945, when a Russian post-mortem on the Führer's body actually proved the first line to be true. We waited with avidity for the disappointing results of the inquest on Goering . . .)

So, did I want a war? Well, I'd spent a long time collecting two sets of cigarette cards – 'Air-raid precautions' and 'Aircraft of the RAF'. And I didn't want to have wasted my time. I didn't want to waste the lovely Spitfires either. And the goodies *always* won – every film and book said so.

Yes, I wanted a war.

Mind made up, I rolled over and slept.

Boy, aged nine, Tyneside

Officers in the uniform of the First World War inspect a new weapon for the Second World War – the mobile searchlight. Later versions rolled on massive rubber tyres – the tiny caterpillar tracks proved hopelessly inadequate.

1939 INDOCTRINATION

My anti-German indoctrination began before I started school. Dad had a set of illustrated 'Great War' books, and on Saturday nights I was put to bed with one of these whilst Mum and Dad went shopping. I studied the pictures in the books avidly and grew up to Kaiser Bill and his murdering legions.

At junior school assembly, we always saluted the Roll of Honour which listed those boys who grew to manhood, only to be killed in France 1914–18. On occasions our headmaster would regale us with stories. I vividly remember his wife standing on the school steps on Empire Day, singing 'Land of Hope and Glory' with all the fervour of the last night of the Proms! To me, all these stories were a continuation of the goodie–baddie theme of Saturday morning movies, the cowboys and Indians.

Boy, aged ten, London

1938–40 INFANT PILGRIMAGE

One Sunday afternoon in the summer of 1938, when I was four, my mother and father went for a walk with my brother in his pram. Trenches were being dug in the streets. My parents had an awful row – my mother kept telling my father it was wrong to volunteer when he had a family. They shouted at each other, my mother cried, so my brother cried too. I stumped along holding on to the pram, wondering what a volunteer was. My grandmother told me later. I wasn't impressed. 'The Germans can't go all over England,' I said.

'You know too much,' she said.

*

In the summer of 1939 my father sent us to Shottery near Stratford. My brother and I caught chicken-pox. We were looked after by a German–Jewish doctor. He taught us how to make animals in plasticine – lions, elephants, horses and camels. He drew ink circles round the last pock-marks on our arms and legs.

We asked him where his children were.

He cried.

I asked my mother why he had cried. 'Don't ask so many questions,' she said.

'He *cried*!' said my brother. Then my mother cried.

We were totally baffled.

After Shottery, we went to my grandmother in Burton-on-Trent. She was very strict, and didn't buy us sweets like our other granny. She smacked us often. One Sunday, my mother came out of her bedroom, looking angry.

'Put your coats on,' she said.

'Where we going?'

'Home,' she said. It was 3 September 1939. We travelled on a train full of soldiers; we were the only civilians. The soldiers were very quiet and smoked a lot. We had to change at Crewe. My brother was thirsty – he wanted milk. They only had Bovril in the buffet. He'd never had it before, and threw a tantrum – he was only three.

When we got home, my mother opened the door, then pushed us back. She grabbed a walking-stick from the hallstand and walked down the passage, where a light showed under the door. Then she jumped through the living-room door, waving the stick. There was my father, holding a large piece of board for blackout. He was frightened out of his wits. I went and put my brother to bed, while they had a terrific row.

We went to Gillingham in Kent next, to be near my father in Chatham Barracks. We were in lodgings. We had an awful old landlady who grumbled all the time. One afternoon my brother went into the garden next door – 'helping', he said. It turned out he had taken the peony buds off every plant. The old man was terribly upset. Peonies only bloom every other year, and they were his pride and joy. The landlady threatened to spank my brother, but my mother sent him to apologize. He came back with two toy soldiers.

In the winter he was playing with his fire-engine one day by the fire. He pushed it too hard. It went into the fire. Going after it, he fell into the fire on both hands. My mother took him to Chatham Naval Hospital. They wanted to cut the blisters off – a new treatment they were using for burnt sailors. My mother said

it was unnatural and looked after my brother's hands herself.
They healed without a scar.

Then came rumours the Germans were going to invade the
South-east. My father said if they blew up the Medway Bridge,
there'd be no reaching London. So at the end of May 1940, he
sent us back to London to be safe . . .

Girl, aged four to six, London

Giving out gasmasks from house to house in early 1939. Most people thought gas would be Hitler's 'secret weapon' – but it was the only thing he failed to use, for fear of reprisals.

Toy manufacturers had a last fling before austerity closed in. Toy steel helmets were on sale just before the war. We preferred real ones when we could get them, despite their appalling weight.

1939 THE ENEMY CHILDREN

'A youth will grow up before which the world will shrink back', promised Adolf Hitler. 'A violently active, dominating, intrepid, brutal youth ... indifferent to pain. No weakness or tenderness in it. I want to see once more in its eyes the gleam ... of a beast of prey.'

The breeding of these killing machines began when a child reached the age of six; he could join the 'Hitler Jugend' as a *Pimpf*. He embarked on a programme of exciting marches, songs, uniforms, fire rituals, solemn oaths of loyalty. Childhood was over. 'Children', declared Baldur von Schirach, Hitler Jugend leader, 'is the term we apply to those non-uniformed creatures of junior age group who have yet to attend an evening parade.' Von Schirach waged war against 'mother's darlings' as vigorously as Dr Rust waged war against education. 'The whole function of education is to create a Nazi.' Every teacher took an oath: 'Adolf Hitler, we swear that we will train the youth of Germany that they will grow up in your ideology, for your aims and purposes.'

Any Hitler Jugend was welcome to report any parent or teacher loath to agree – the child owed them no loyalty. His duty lay only to his Führer and comrades. 'Youth must be led by youth. Young Folk Boys are tough, silent, loyal. Young Folk Boys are comrades. Honour is supreme' was one vow parroted by every ten-year-old.

Girlhood had a different destiny – to serve and breed. 'The lowest type of male is infinitely higher than the noblest female', opined a sex manual. The only task was 'to develop out of the love of these girls a completely unconditional devotion to the Führer. Everything else is negligible.'

More practically, the function of German girls was to produce new crops of Youth, preferably male. 'Lifelong monogamy is perverse. There are plenty of willing and qualified youths ready to unite with the girls. Fortunately, one boy of good race suffices for twenty girls.' To encourage the new crop, girls were sent to labour camps in close proximity to boys' camps. Those who became pregnant were praised and could leave their offspring in state nursery schools to be raised as Hitler's Children.

The weird mixture of spartan discipline and promiscuity brought confusion. The society that gave a medal to the lad who reported that his father had thrashed him for getting a girl pregnant (the father was sent to a concentration camp) produced a host of disturbed adolescents. They cluttered the juvenile courts, rebellious not only against parental and school discipline (which they had been trained to be) but surprisingly indifferent to Nazi ideals – they listened to American Jazz and formed themselves into bands with such names as the 'Harlem Club'. An S S security report concluded sadly: 'Their ideal is democratic freedom and American laxity.'

German children were placed in classrooms as spies; one teacher was executed for permitting a child with a hurt arm to fail to give the Nazi salute.

The War Papers *(Marshall Cavendish), no. 27*

After Munich 1938: Mr Chamberlain bleating about 'peace in our time' with his wretched little piece of paper. It carried Hitler's signature guaranteeing peace . . .

The old news-vendor could be a revenant from the First World War – only the buses and clothes make it 1939.

CHAPTER 2 **FIRST DAYS OF WAR**

1939 **THE DAY WAR BROKE OUT**

Mr Chamberlain's broadcast was not impressive. I remembered him from the newsreels, coming out of his aeroplane after Munich, waving his little piece of paper and promising 'peace in our time'. I thought he looked like a sheep, and now he bleated like a sheep. He talked about notes being sent and replies not being received. He *regretted* that a state of war now existed between Great Britain and Germany. He sounded really *hurt*, like Hitler was some shiftless council tenant who had failed to pay his rent after faithfully promising to do so.

That wasn't the way to talk to Hitler; he should be threatening to kick his teeth in . . . I knew there'd be trouble . . .

There was. The sirens went immediately. We didn't know what to do. We had no shelters; nothing but little gasmasks in cardboard boxes. We went to the front windows and stared out. Everything was peaceful and sunny. Old Charlie Brown, who hadn't worked for years with his bad chest, after being gassed on the Somme, was marching round the square, sticking his chest out. Wearing his best suit and medals from the Last Lot. He looked determined, but ridiculous. Mam said he had volunteered to be a warden yesterday, and obviously felt he should do *something*.

Dad said 'If he sounds his rattle, that means poison gas – put your gasmask on.'

I said 'He hasn't *got* a rattle.'

The world seemed broken in half. The earth, the houses, roses, sunlit trees were still England. But the air was suddenly German; there wasn't a Spitfire or a Hurricane, or even a Gloster Gladiator in sight. Soon, like on the newsreels from Spain, the air would fill with the orderly black crosses of German bombers, with endless strings of tiny bombs falling from their bellies. And only Charlie Brown to stop them. I couldn't stand still – I went into my bedroom and considered trying to pray, a thing I hadn't done for years. It didn't seem much use against Nazi bombers. The Spaniards must have been great prayers, being Catholics, and it hadn't done them much good . . . I decided to keep my eyes wide open instead.

My old teddy-bear was sitting in the corner; I hadn't spared him a glance in years, but now he looked at me, appealingly.

I put him under my bed for safety.

Then the all-clear sounded.

Charlie Brown headed straight for the Cannon Inn and downed several pints double-quick.

Boy, aged nine, Tyneside

1939   IN THE BEGINNING

I remember my parents listening to Neville Chamberlain's voice on the wireless. He sounded grave and my parents looked serious, so I hurried out into the garden in a mood of mingled awe and excitement.

Not being a typically bloodthirsty little boy, I had only the sketchiest idea of what war would mean. The few notions I had came from my father's stories about his life in the trenches as a Medical Corps corporal in the First World War – stories with all the gory bits carefully left out. I had somewhere at the back of my mind vague thoughts of knights in armour and medieval sieges. At any rate the one thing that was clear to me was that some day quite soon our house might be surrounded by enemy soldiers.

We should have to lock the doors and, in that case, we would need plenty of firewood. So I did my bit for the War Effort by marching to the coalhouse, fetching a little axe and vigorously chopping up a small wooden box. It didn't occur to me that, by the same reasoning, perhaps I should have shifted our entire stock of coal into the kitchen.

Boy, aged ten, Manchester

1939   FALSE ALARM

It was the first day of the war, when the siren went off in Newcastle. It was a false alarm, but it was received by the local coal mine. My brother-in-law, who was working as a roadman, was warned by the pit that there would probably be a gas attack and was told to go and inform his family to take gas precautions.

I was at their home at the time and we all set to, barred and sealed all the doors and windows, pushed pillows up the chimneys, stocked the food and water into the bedroom. My sister's baby was only a few months old, and we had to install her in a gasproof cot. This had to be pumped with air. My sister was new to the device and we were all terrified in case the baby should get too much or too little air. My sister's face was like death. We were all gathered together in the bedroom terrified, waiting for news over two hours, before we learnt it was all a false alarm. We were ill for days after. Then we had to replace the food, etc. back down a long flight of stairs, haul down the soot-stained pillows from the chimney and clean them ready for bedtime. Our legs were worn out tracking up and down the stairs.

Girl, aged fifteen, Hexham

The nurse has a superior gasmask and steel helmet. The baby is almost totally enclosed inside his. The photograph was taken at Esher in Surrey.

'Uncle Mac' – Donald McCulloch in action. He did as much to steady the younger end of the nation with his Children's Hour broadcasts as Tommy Handley or Winston Churchill.

3 SEPT
1939   CHILDREN'S HOUR

I had no idea what the word 'war' meant, nor why I said 'I hope there won't be a war, mummy.'

She made no reply; I was not reassured. A few minutes later, the Prime Minister's voice was heard on the radio. The dreadful unknown war had just begun. I was desperate. I went out into the street, in search of comfort. I found nothing but the fear on people's faces.

Later, I sat alone on the stairs. What did it mean? What would happen to us? It was very dark on the stairs.

Through the wall came the sound of Children's Hour. Larry the Lamb, Dennis the Dachshund, Uncle Mac, David Davies, Aunty Doris, Aunty Muriel, Romany ...

It would be all right. As long as there was Children's Hour, it would be all right if I held on tight.

They did not let me down.

Girl, aged nine, Cheshire

1939   HOLY SOLACE

It was Sunday morning and we had all been to Mass. It was also the Sunday that the priest was due to call for our contribution to church funds. (In those days, either the Parish Priest or his curate called once a month.) Anyway, Father Daly called and, having had a cup of tea and a biscuit, he and my mum talked about the news just broadcast.

There were five of us children, and my eldest brother was only eleven, but we were all upset when our mum said to Father Daly that her sons would all be cannon-fodder. (What it means is the waste cotton-wool that was used in the guns in the First World War.) However, Father Daly comforted my mother by telling her the war wouldn't last long, and that my brothers were too young to be conscripted.

Girl, Liverpool

1939   THE SINKING OF THE *ATHENIA*

We were sitting on a hatch feeling sick when we were blown up into the air. I wasn't hurt but mother hurt her shoulder. After we were blown in the air we were put in a lifeboat. I climbed into it myself. Then we were out on the ocean all night. Nobody said very much, and there was no singing or laughing or crying.

Survivors rescued from the torpedoed Athenia. This sinking, of an unarmed liner, within hours of the outbreak of war, confirmed the war in our minds as a crusade against slinking cowards. Throughout the war, the U-boats were thought 'cowardly', as opposed to our 'heroic' British submarines, though by 1940 both were following exactly the same 'sink on sight' tactics.

We saw a battleship and climbed on to it up a ladder. The sailors were very kind to us and we were taken to Greenock in Scotland. Mother was in hospital for eight days with her shoulder but I was up and around.

Rosie Ralph, aged ten

LETTER TO A SAILOR

242 Linsmore Crescent, East York, Toronto
Nov. 1st 1939

Dear Dennis,

I was waiting til I got home before I wrote to you. Don't mind if I don't call you Uncle Dennis, it sounds too old. I am very glad to be home again. Soon as I got home my Dad bought me a canary. It sings good, too.

I was scared going home. I never got undressed once going home until we reached land and was sailing up the St Lawrence. I took my shoes off, of course.

When I got home my dog Buddie didn't even know me. I went back to school the day after I got home. I hope you have been busy sinking all the German submarines. It is not very cold here. Don't forget to send that picture that you promised. I want my brother to see how good-looking you are. He won't believe me when I tell him. How are all the other sailors on your ship? Tell them I often think of them. I would just like to come and see you and have tea with you, but not the same way I came before. Hope you are all fine,

Love and x x x x x x
ROSIE RALPH.

1939 UNREALITY

My father got a copy of the *Daily Express* war map, which we hung on the kitchen wall and decorated with little coloured flags representing the Allied and German forces. It was good fun, but quite unreal – as unreal as the popular songs on the wireless.

We're going to hang out the washing on the Siegfried Line,
Have you any dirty washing, Mother dear?
We're going to hang out the washing on the Siegfried Line
For the washing day is here,

Whether the weather may be wet or fine,
We will hang it out, without a care,
We're going to hang out the washing on the Siegfried Line
If the Siegfried Line's still there!

Boy, aged ten, Manchester

1939 BUILDING A DUG-OUT

My father excavated a hole in the tennis court for a dug-out, covered with tree-trunks supporting corrugated iron and topped with several feet of earth.

Boy, aged ten, London

SEPT–DEC
1939 LOOKING FOR THE WAR

They cancelled school immediately 'for the Duration of the Emergency'. Handy; I had a lot to do. There was the map of Europe, given away free with the first copy of *War Weekly*, to pin on my bedroom wall; lots of little flags to cut out: British, French, German and, bafflingly, Russian. I also hung up score-charts of German ships sunk, planes shot down, tanks destroyed.

Then me and Stanley set off on our bikes to look for the war. Somebody said they were desperate for people to fill sandbags at Preston Hospital, to protect the windows, so we dashed down there. Unfortunately, the hospital porter turned out to be old Jack Dawson, our bossy neighbour. He turned us back at the gate, saying he didn't want a lot of bloody kids hanging about the place. We considered reporting him to the police, for sabotaging the War Effort.

We worked out ways of fooling German bombers. If they machine-gunned us from the air, we'd pretend to fall down dead, then get up and run again, then pretend to die again. This would ruin their estimate of civilian casualties.

We lived on our bikes, looking for Defences, which seemed in perilously short supply. Every little bit of barbed wire went down in our notebooks, even the thin strands round farmers' fields, which didn't really count but we put them down just the same. Then *real* Defences appeared – single pom-poms on the Bank Top; armed trawlers. We inspected them daily, looking for improvements, and making sure the crews knew their job. Best were the barrage balloons. We spent hours at Dockwray Square, staring through the railings; the balloon was like a great silver elephant, whose sides crinkled with every breeze. In the evenings, the RAF crew played football with us, till the girls came, then they lost all interest in football. We thought of reporting them to the police, for neglecting the War Effort. Playing football with us kept them fit; but daft giggling girls were sure to ruin their morale . . .

Then they restarted school, mornings only. We still couldn't actually *go* to school, because they hadn't built its air-raid shelters yet. Our class, only, met in the old winding-house of Preston Colliery; a huge dank brick underground arch that smelt evilly of cats. That winding-house was our air-raid shelter. Later in the war, it sustained a near-miss from a very small bomb, and collapsed, killing forty. On fine days, we wandered round the town in a crocodile, looking for a place to sit down together. We usually ended up in Preston Cemetery, sitting on the tombstones, doing sums. Stanley reckoned this was so that if there was an air raid, and we got killed by bombs, we could be buried immediately, without being taken home first.

Later, our school was flattened by a land-mine, also the Rex Cinema next door. The Rex manager, a good bloke who told us jokes and made us laugh at Saturday morning matinees, was killed outright. The headmaster and the nastiest teacher in the school, Miss Townsend, were buried for hours in the wreckage, but dug out unharmed. We were outraged. We all wished *they'd* been killed, instead of the Rex manager, because they were both terrible caners and complete Nazi sadists. Miss Townsend actually had blonde hair coiled in plaits round her head and thick muscular legs just like the Hitler Youth Mädchen. My mother wondered what they'd been up to, fire-watching in the school on their own . . .

Unfortunately we were transferred to Spring Gardens School immediately, all classes having to sit together in the hall, with the Spring Gardens kids peering in at us and laughing, like we were something in a zoo.

Stanley was evacuated to Hexham, but returned after a fortnight. Some Hexham kids pushed him backwards into a cowpat. The woman he was billeted with didn't wash his blazer, and he had to go to school with the dry cowpat stuck to him, and she didn't clean his shoes or make his bed or anything. And the teacher kept remarking how scruffy town kids were. So he came home; he said it was all cows and cowpats and *boring*.

It was becoming increasingly hard to find any way of beating Hitler. We even volunteered to help knit comforts for the troops. We would hold the hanks of wool before us, on outstretched hands, while the girls wound it into balls. They were very bossy,

Their school closed for lack of shelters, this class of boys at the Royal Cross Deaf and Dumb School, Preston, try to learn in the semi-darkness of an old industrial boiler. The boiler had been in a wood in the school grounds for about fifty years. It was cleaned, creosoted and fitted with a door to make a shelter for thirty pupils.

constantly shouting at us 'Hold your hands *up*, can't you?' Then the vicar's wife got sarky about the quality of our mums' knitting, announcing 'We are trying to knit *comforts* for the troops, my dears, not *discomforts*.' So most of the mums gave it up in a huff. My Mum gave me the Balaclava helmet instead.

Dad joined the wardens. They had one interesting night in our square, practising putting out real incendiary bombs with sand. They had to summon the ambulance; the wardens were so enthusiastic, everyone got their eyes full of sand, and they took the bomb-fins away, so we couldn't have them for souvenirs. All that the wardens did otherwise was hold a Saturday night whist-drive-and-dance for their funds. I was put in charge of lemonade selling. I sold an incredible amount of lemonade, ginger pop and American ice cream soda; I learnt to play whist and won the booby prize, and I learnt ballroom-dancing. But it didn't seem to have a lot to do with beating Hitler.

Perhaps Hitler was already beaten. The German pocket-battleship *Graf Spee* ran away from three very small British cruisers, and scuttled herself in Montevideo harbour, though she had suffered little damage except a shell in her bakery. The German captain said his crew could not fight on without a supply of fresh bread, and shot himself. To us kids, if the Germans were all like the *Graf Spee*, there didn't seem a lot to beat.

Boy, aged ten, Tyneside

CHAPTER 3   EVACUATION

1939   GREY SQUIRRELS

When we were evacuated, we went to a massive manor owned by Lady Bibby. She was a fantastic woman, but she hated grey squirrels. She kept a gun under the window and every time she saw one she shot it dead.

Boy, aged eight, Liverpool

1939   EVACUEE'S FIRST POSTCARD HOME

Dear Mum, I hope you are well. I don't like the man's face much. Perhaps it will look better in daylight. I like the dog's face best.

1940   WOLF-CUB

Even at eleven, this picture wouldn't have fooled me. It was propaganda, meant to point out what we were soon taught to call 'our war-aims'. Still, if obvious propaganda would help to beat Adolf ... we churned out 'war-aims' posters in school like billy-ho! I won a prize for one: I still squirm at the memory of its crassness.

My first recollection was the arrival of the 'Vackies' as we nick-named them. I was a cub with Witton Church Group and the Patrol Leader informed us that evacuees from Liverpool and Manchester were arriving on Saturday at Northwich Station and we were to assist in helping with baggage, etc. and with the relocation of these unfortunate families. Trainloads arrived regularly. They were met at the station and taken to Station Road Chapel. Hot drinks, sandwiches, biscuits, etc. were handed out and each child was carrying their sole possessions in a suitcase or parcels, the regulation gasmask and an identity-tag. The cubs were soon busy helping to organize, bringing small groups to the chapel, serving cups of tea or cocoa, taking messages or assisting small children on to the coaches that were laid on to take them to their final destination. Some children treated it as a great adventure, others sat silently, scarcely able to take in the scene, others quietly sobbed as they were handed over to foster-mothers. In some cases children were re-located with their mothers, possibly they had been blitzed out of their homes, as we could see the red glow of fires in the skies over Merseyside and Manchester and hear in the far distance the thuds of the explosions as these cities were razed to the ground.

Boy, aged ten, Cheshire

Evacuation – middle class – was a great adventure. Used to being away from home, they revelled in what seemed a year-long holiday in West Country hotels.

1939 EVACUATION – MIDDLE CLASS

In the case of this group there were no tearful farewells. They were already many miles from their parents, and they were with their friends. They travelled in two charabancs, taking with them a few members of staff and one of the joint headmistresses. They were bound for Woolacombe, a holiday resort in North Devon, which was an idyllic situation. They had lessons in the morning and in the afternoon they were free to do as they liked. They could go anywhere in threes – one to have an accident, one to stay with her and one to run for help. There are three miles of sand at Woolacombe and swimming was much more interesting than it had been in the swimming pool at Reigate.

The countryside held exciting walks, either along the coast or inland up the donkey-track which was the old smugglers' path, used for carrying their brandy and rum.

In September, the rest of the school was evacuated; they took over four hotels.

Girl, aged twelve, Devon

1939 EVACUATION – WORKING CLASS

We left home early in the morning, with our gasmasks hanging round our necks. It was very dark. We got to the school and all the mothers looked very grim. They were trying not to cry but one or two of them did. We didn't cry because we didn't really know what was happening to us.

When we reached the end of our journey we all climbed out

The working-class were not so sure . . .

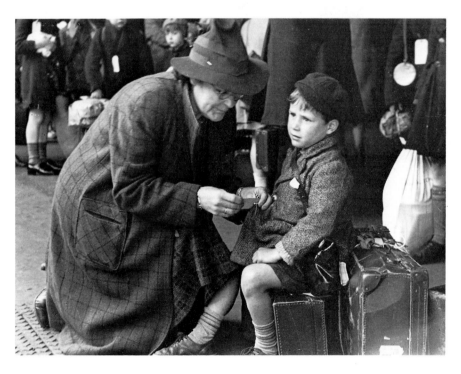

and went to a church hall. Then we found out that we'd come to the wrong place ... we'd gone to where the boys should have been. But no one could be bothered to change us over. We were taken to a nice place with a very, very old couple. The house was old and stood by a lake, which was full of rotting conkers that smelt terrible. I was lucky because I was with my friend Mavis. In the evening we told each other creepy stories so that we were very frightened. We soon discovered a room that was full of apples. When everybody was asleep, we crept along the passage and got some. But we didn't always succeed. The floor-boards creaked and we thought someone would hear. When we did get apples, we took them back to eat in bed.

A few weeks later, the old man died. Then we were moved to different houses. I went to a house with people who went on organized stealing-trips into Redhill, and they tried to make me go with them.

After a while I got rheumatic fever. I was quite ill but I didn't like to tell anybody. One morning I went to school and collapsed in class and was taken to Earlswood Common Hospital. When I got there I was put straight into a hot bed – it had an electric blanket – which I'd never heard of. At the hospital they had a [wind-up] gramophone. They kept playing songs like 'Any Um-barellas' and 'Hang out the washing on the Siegfried Line'.

In a bed next to me was a poor Jewish girl who had escaped from Vienna. She was very upset because she didn't know what had happened to her parents.

Then our army had to retreat at Dunkirk. All the hospitals were preparing for that, so they sent me home in an ambulance.

I'd only been at home a few days when I picked up the paper and saw the big black letters saying PARIS HAS FALLEN and I couldn't really believe it.

And then came the bombing of London.

Girl, Surrey

... but a bag of sweets was some consolation ...

1940 ROMANCE

We were quite well-off during the war. We lived in a bigger house than all the other kids. But we weren't rich or anything. I was a spoilt child and got nearly everything I asked for.

We lived in Warrington; there were a lot of factories there, so the town was bombed quite a lot. Because of this, my mother sent me to live with my hard-up aunty in Yorkshire.

At first I was very unsettled – it was so different; in Warrington I'd had lots of friends. It was just like being born again. I missed

. . . for being sorted like parcels . . .

my mother a lot, because we were very close. I cried a lot. My aunt called me a soppy spoilt little baby.

I had to do a lot of work, so hard that when I lay down in her bed at night I fell asleep almost straight away. I never had time to read the books I brought with me. I was also made to go to Mass, though I wasn't a Catholic.

I did not meet any children my own age, till I'd been at the cottage a year, and it was a boy. I did not like boys, especially dirty, smelly, scruffy ones like this Mark. He used to live in Weymouth, but his father had bought a little farm down the lane just past the shops.

Every time I went to the shops for my aunty, I used always to see Mark. After a few weeks he used to come round with his father. Because my uncle and his father were good friends, we too became good friends after a bit. Somehow I did not seem to mind the smelliness of Mark. When he came for Sunday dinner, I always went for a walk with him in the woods near by.

But the war ended. I was a much older woman by then. I did not want to leave the village, not because of my aunty, but because of Mark. I think I was in love with him.

I must remain anonymous; my husband must not find out.

... getting washed in public in funny bowls in funny great houses ...

1939 BEING AMONG THE CHOSEN

When we arrived in Portmadoc we were taken to the Town Hall – where people chose which children they would look after. My sister Pat was very attractive, whereas I was rather plain. An old man noticed Pat and asked a teacher if he could take her. She told him that she had a sister, and if he wanted her he must take me too. He went home to ask his wife if she could have two children. She agreed, so he returned to collect us. When he arrived I started to cry and refused to go. The old man went to the nearest florist and bought an enormous bunch of flowers for me. We finally arrived at the old man's house seated in a chauffeur-driven car. At the house there was a big library. Pat used to spend hours upon hours in the library.

... and sleeping in rows on cold and highly polished floors ...

Then I caught chicken-pox and we had to go to another house.

At the second house was a very strict woman. Now I really liked ginger and one day this woman made some ginger-cakes. When the woman went to have her afternoon sleep I sneaked into the kitchen and picked round one of the cakes. When I looked at the cakes, I saw the one I'd picked stood out like a sore thumb. So I picked round all the cakes to make them look the same. When the woman woke up and saw the cakes she sat all the children on the floor and looked for the child with the guilty-looking face. When she caught me she took me off and locked me in a dark attic.

Pat had written to our mum a few days before. She said in our letter that we both wanted to go home. My mum came to collect us while I was still in the attic. When the woman explained why I was in the attic, my mum went mad. She took us straight away.

Girl, aged four, Liverpool

1939 A LONDON EVACUEE SEES HIS FIRST COW

The cow is a mamal. It has six sides, right, left, an upper and below. At the back is a tail, on which hangs a brush. With this it sends the flies away so they do not fall into the milk. The head is for the purpose of growing horns and so that the mouth can be somewhere. The horns are to butt with, and the mouth is to moo with. Under the cow hangs the milk. It is arranged for milking. When people milk, the milk comes and there is never an end to the supply. How the cow does it I have not realized but it makes more and more. The cow has a fine sense of smell; one can smell it far away. This is the reason for the fresh air in the country.

The man cow is called an ox. It is not a mamal. The cow does not eat much but what it eats, it eats twice so that it gets enough. When it is hungry it moos and when it says nothing it is because all its inside is full up with grass.

BBC news, 29 October 1939

1939 EVACUATION TO FOLKESTONE

First we were evacuated to Deal. There I was billeted at the Rectory. The house and food were all right but the people were snobbish blue-blooded Tories. The Rector himself was not objectionable, but his wife was the typical old-fashioned Rector's wife, and very Victorian. The Rectory is the biggest house in Deal, yet they only took in four children. There were seven large rooms in the house which were not used. Yet the lady of the house complained that four children were too much for her to manage (her maid did all the work) and said that Sheila and I would have to move to another billet.

There was no school at Deal so we were moved to Folkestone. At Folkestone the billeting authorities moved us all into large hotels. Directly we were in they started moving us out into private billets. I was in a lovely hotel, Barelle House. We were treated exactly as guests; we had the same meals as the hotel visitors. Mrs Godefroy the proprietress treated us so well that she

EVACUATION
OF
WOMEN AND CHILDREN
FROM LONDON, Etc.

FRIDAY, 1st SEPTEMBER.

Up and Down business trains as usual, with few exceptions.

Main Line and Suburban services will be curtailed while evacuation is in progress during the day.

SATURDAY & SUNDAY,
SEPTEMBER 2nd & 3rd.

The train service will be exactly the same as on Friday.

Remember that there will be very few Down Mid-day business trains on Saturday.

SOUTHERN RAILWAY

... at some inconvenience to the City gents ...

... even if you had to carry all your clothes in a cardboard box ...

49

... and be haunted by the Ministry of Information disguised as the ubiquitous Adolf. In spite of this poster, most children were back in the big cities in time for the Blitz.

went bankrupt and had to close the hotel. We found out later that she had been using her own private funds to feed us as the billeting money does not nearly pay.

From there we were moved to this hotel and were told, 'It won't be for long, you'll be moved out soon.' We have been here almost a month. The first few days at the Victoria were the worst I have ever experienced. I never knew what it is like to feel hungry before. We were reduced to eating anything, lumps of dry bread, cake crumbs, etc. (Mrs Godefroy used to let us come back to Barelle House for food; she used to give us cups of tea, plates of chips, apples and all manner of good things.)

We told our mistresses we had not enough to eat. As a result the hotel people called us liars and other things not fit to write. We protested so strongly that now our food is quite good. I feel certain that the hotel people must make a profit out of us, though. We have no milk except in powdered form, then it is a very little in our tea. We have no eggs or fresh food; it is all tinned. One day we did have eggs but they were pickled ones and nearly all rotten.

They are gradually moving us out; of course, the older ones will be moved last so I have a long time to wait. I am thoroughly sick of so much uncertainty; we will not be really settled down till Christmas. As they move us out, they move elementary children in. Of course, these are younger and not old enough to complain about food etc. The evacuation scheme in Folkestone is rotten. Over 1,000 children have gone home.

We are a long way from school here, over two miles. We first climb about 150 steps to the top of the cliff, and then uphill to school. We cannot get back to the hotel for dinner; they do not keep us any hot at the hotel so we must have it at school. This costs 10d. each. We have had continuous rain here this week and have had to ride to school. The fares are 2d. each way, so you can guess how difficult it is for mother to keep up with all the expenses.

When we got up this morning, the kitchen was flooded out – eight inches of water, so we went to school with very little breakfast. During the day the rain continued and the water rose. The men were wading about in water past their knees. We could have no cooked dinner as the gas stove was partly under water. You see we are right at the foot of a very steep cliff which the water simply pours down. In some of the hotels along the front the tables and chairs were floating about.

Another trouble in this hotel is infection. One girl caught a cold and practically the whole house went down with colds. A girl got impetigo, then a boy caught it. Both went to hospital.

I have got past the stage of caring what food we have, etc. now though.

I console myself with talking Communism, reading Communism and thinking Communism all the time.

Girl, aged sixteen

1941 PERKS

During Liverpool's heaviest bombing, my two brothers and I were evacuated to a small town in Wales. Since I was the oldest, I took charge. A lady asked us if we had any pyjamas or slippers. Since we did not I ordered two sets of pyjamas for my brothers and two nightdresses for myself, thinking I was getting them free off the government.

At the end of the war, when we returned home, my Mum gave me a big walloping because every week till the end of the war she had to pay bills for socks, underwear, pyjamas, shirts and jumpers. As well as paying for our things my Mum also paid for everyone else's in our school, because I was also ordering things for my friends and then swapping them for sweets.

Girl, aged twelve, Liverpool

1940–41 A LOVE OF COUNTRY LIFE

We marched from our schools to the station, complete with gasmask and lapel labels. The streets were lined with our families. Going down Nile Street, my grandmother ran into the road-way to say farewell. The police lining the route tried to stop her, but though she was tiny she bulldozed her way through and marched with us to the station. We had one teacher in each compartment in charge of twelve pupils. When the train departed, the wailing and tears echoed up and down the train.

At Morpeth, Joyce and myself were last to be housed. At nine p.m., feeling hungry and dejected, Miss Holmes took us and bought chips. After a short time, Joyce was moved to Wooler and I went to Alnham, a hamlet consisting of a pele tower, Anglo-Saxon church, school, Memorial Hall, a few houses and ancient earthworks. We lived in the Memorial Hall; part was curtained off to make a sleeping area and the rest was a common-room. Thirty children lived there, with a resident matron and cook. We attended the school, where I first encountered Miss Black, the schoolmistress. The schoolhouse garden followed the road down to the Memorial Hall; there was a cucumber-frame. In one of our gardening periods, an Alnham lad demolished it, and unfortunately I carried the blame, and was punished. This started the feud between Miss Black and myself.

After the Memorial Hall closed, I went to the Wilson family at Scrainwood. Mrs Wilson was a first-class cook and had a huge pile of awards from country shows. Mr Wilson was a bedridden invalid, from a stroke. The living-room had a black-leaded stove and boiler with tap; a high-backed settle kept draughts off you when sitting at the fire. Paraffin lamps for light were mounted on the wall. Cooking was done by a paraffin oven which left the smell of burnt paraffin every time it was used. Sticky fly-papers hung everywhere.

Scrainwood was a backwater, consisting of the Big House surrounded by barns, byre, stores, hay-shed and workshop. The most impressive waterwheel was in a section normally kept locked for safety. Within ten feet of the wheel the noise was deafening. The wheel turned continually but I have no recollection of it having any end-product. Next was the stables – four shire-horses worked the farm. At right-angles were two cottages. Two brothers called Snaith lived in one, typical hill-shepherds, able to cook, knit, doing all the tasks to survive country life. One kept ferrets for hunting rabbits. When going rabbiting he would shout to me 'Eck, 'ere!' At this call he expected me to join him. He never spoke to me till the work started, then I joined in learning to ferret, snare, net and drive the rabbits out of the

At its best, evacuation could be a mind-blowing adventure. The steam traction engine was a casualty of the war: it was replaced in 1944 by the massive Fordson tractor.

warrens. After he killed them, I would gut them and nick their back legs together, and pair them for carrying. A butcher called once a week and took the catch to sell.

During summer, Mr Snaith would dispose of wasps' nests by smoking them out and burning them. He was also an expert on stick-dressing (making ornamental shepherd's crooks).

Our water was carried from a tap in buckets. Washing-water was drawn from the burn that passed by the house. At the rear were the outhouses; first the pigsty: each family had at least one fattening-pig. Second the woodshed, used for cutting and storing logs, storing paraffin, pig-feed, hen-feed, tools. Last the netty, or earth-closet, which tipped on to the open ash-pit behind. Every spring the men would dig out the ash-pits and spread them on the fields before ploughing.

When the time arrived for killing the pig, a tripod of three poles was erected at the end of the cottages. This hung the carcass for scraping and butchering. The pig's head was hung on the back door, as was the custom. The joints were cut and salted, then hung in the larder for use in the following months. Sausage was made from the offal, using the intestine for skins. Other winter preparations included bottling eggs and fruit, making jam and digging the potato-pit.

The 1941 winter was very bad; we were unable to attend school for six weeks because of the snow. At one time it totally covered the cottage. Work was restricted to the farmyard, the animals having been brought in before the snow fell. Winter entertainment was considerable; the Wilsons were into country dance music. The two eldest lads played accordions, Tom the drums. Many a good night was had with their friends, Mrs Wilson providing the food and all playing till the early hours.

It was winter when we had ice-cream. Ice was taken off the rain-barrels, crushed and mixed with milk, sugar, cornflour, served on dishes in front of the fire.

During the summer we helped with the harvest, threshing corn with the steam-engines and thresher. Pulling turnips gave us the reward of riding the farm-horses from the field with loads of turnips.

The big event of the week was meeting the weekly bus. It arrived every Saturday at nine a.m. en route for Rothbury. When it returned at eight, the locals met it; long discussions were had with the passengers, relaying news of the area. I often wondered what time the driver finished! It was also a parcel-delivery service.

We walked to school each day, taking sandwiches for lunch. Miss Black taught five-year-olds to fourteen-year-olds, all in the same room. In winter it was heated by a pot-bellied stove in the front. The evacuees sat at the back, far away from it. My mother sent me a corduroy jacket to wear. It had a strong smell and Miss Black made me hang it outside to get rid of the smell. I protested bitterly because of the cold, but it fell on deaf ears. I put up with this a few days, then decided to give up school. I used to go up into the fields, passing the time with the ploughmen. Eventually, Mrs Wilson found out. First her lads tried to take me to school, but I escaped. Then Mrs Wilson tried, with the same results. The final result was a letter home, and the end of evacuation, aged eight. Living at Scrainwood gave me a love of country life which has had a profound influence ever since.

Boy, aged six, North Shields

1939–40 THE END OF EVACUATION

I began to get bored – here we were at war and nothing was happening. The standard of eating in the country was lower than I was used to at home. Mum and Dad visited me at weekends bringing food parcels; the thought of returning home with them was very provoking. In London were hundreds of barrage balloons, shelters were being built, sandbags were everywhere. The pace was what I was missing, as well as my home.

My twelfth birthday was spent in West Peckham and the following Sunday, heartily homesick, I asked my parents to take me back with them.

London was, for me, like a return from exile. My pet cat met me at the gate, the neighbours welcomed me and the sun shone. Even my brother did not seem to find me so objectionable.

There were no schools open, but the local vicar arranged a class in his house, using local retired people with some teaching experience to help out. I joined this class which at least kept us off the streets. We learnt odd subjects such as Esperanto and Monopoly, all very enjoyable! The classes were ten to fifteen in number, and at least ensured there was a sprinkling of youngsters in the congregation on Sundays.

Boy, aged ten, London

56

CHAPTER 4 **THE PHONEY WAR**

1939 THE FIRST RAID

The first raid came as we were sitting down to dinner. When the sirens went we left everything and ran down the shelter.

I sat at the shelter door and stared at the sunlit path only inches from my nose, thinking 'In here it's safe, but out there is Danger.' I couldn't resist putting a finger out into Danger, like it was a bowl of hot water. Nothing happened, so I put my whole hand out, whereupon Mam clouted me for mucking about. I saw a beetle crawling on the path, in Danger. It seemed quite unworried. I imagined a huge piece of shrapnel coming down and squashing it flat. But the beetle would never know it was in Danger, and it still wouldn't know when it was squashed flat. So for the beetle, war didn't exist. And the birds were singing as well, and I felt stupid cowering in this hole, and wondered why wars were only for People.

Then Mam started worrying about the meal getting cold on the table, worrying the dog might eat it. So she nipped out and fetched the sausage and chips and we ate them. Then she went back for the bread and butter, and finally the prunes and custard, and then to make a cup of tea. The whole shelter was full of dirty washing-up and it was embarrassing because Mrs Spedding and Brian hadn't had their dinner yet, and there wasn't enough for them. But Mam gave them a cup of tea.

War on a shoe-string: house as fire-station, taxi as fire-engine. The only things there seemed plenty of were sandbags and courage. The sandbags protected the windows: nothing protected the roof. But were we downhearted? No!

Mam was just thinking about nipping out to do the washing-up, and worrying about her two o'clock appointment at the hairdressers when the guns started, out to sea. The guns got nearer, like thunder, then worse than thunder. Like the sky was cracking in half.

Then we heard people shouting. Not screaming, but shouting like a football crowd, only scattered over the whole district. Then the people in the next shelter.

'Kill the bugger – get him – get him.' They were outside their shelter, so I nipped out, and there was the German bomber streaking up the river, so long and thin you could tell it was a Dornier Flying Pencil. And bursts of anti-aircraft fire, like grey balls of cotton wool growing in the sky, in clumps of four, but all miles behind the bomber.

The man next door was jumping up and down on top of his shelter, screaming his head off. 'Get yer eyes chaarked, ye stupid buggers,' he was shouting at the gunners. 'What ye think ye're paid for?' Like they were the referee at a football match . . .

'Mind yer language in front o' that bairn, Jack!' said his wife, but he took no notice.

When the gunners missed again, you could hear the whole district groaning, like a football crowd. The man next door began pulling his plants up, he was so mad. Then when there was another set of bangs he would look up, then cover up his eyes, saying he couldn't bear to look.

Just as the bomber seemed to be getting away, it flew right into a cluster of grey cotton wool, and came out the other side as a mass of bits. God, you should've heard the cheering. Like Newcastle United had scored the winning goal for the F A Cup. It echoed and echoed.

Then the man next door said: 'They were brave lads for Germans. They flew in a straight line and didn't run away.' There were tears in his eyes. And everybody else began saying how brave the German airmen had been, and what a terrible thing war was.

But you could tell they were thoroughly enjoying themselves, really.

Boy, aged nine, Tyneside

1939 MUNITIONS

In 1939 I worked in a munition factory in Kirkby. I was about eighteen. I worked on the night-shift, from ten till six next morning. I worked in the TNT room. We had to wear protective clothing, e.g. white hat, three-quarter-length jacket and white trousers in coarse flannel and hard white shoes. Each night before we started work we had to cross over a barrier which searched you to see if you had cigarettes and matches on you.

Women making ammunition belts for machine-guns, probably to be used in the first RAF night bombers.

If you got through the barrier you were clean, so could get on with your work. My job was cleaning bomb casings.

Girl, aged eighteen, Liverpool

I left school in 1939. It was late August. The S S *Ceramic* was about to sail from Gladstone Dock. I had to deliver a parcel to my father, who was a stoker. I was about to go home when I heard they were looking for a deck-boy. The bosun asked me, and I went there and then, little realizing a Great War was looming over us.

Before we reached our first port, Tenerife, we got a message from the Admiralty for all ships to meet at Sierra Leone.

Later, as we left Australia we heard from the wireless that the *Doric Star* had been sunk and we were ordered to pick up survivors.

The *Graf Spee* spotted us, and chased us through the Indian Ocean. But we escaped and joined the convoy at Sierra Leone for the journey home.

We had just reached Africa and on deck I saw these two ladies staring at a wrecked lifeboat. One of the ladies was a stewardess. She said to the other lady, 'Let's go and pray in your cabin.' I watched them slowly walk away and I never saw them again. I gathered it was somebody she knew.

We were the first convoy of the war at Liverpool, arriving January 1940, about three weeks overdue.

Father kept me at home, saying I was too young for such hazards. I should have sailed on the ship my father lost his life on. He kept going and finally lost his life in December 1942.

Boy, aged fourteen, Liverpool

1939–40 WAR AT SCAPA FLOW

5 Sept. There was a German submarine in Scapa Flow before we declared war, but as it had done no damage they could do nothing about it. Three spies were caught on Mainland.

6 Sept. There's excitement enough now! This morning we heard the drone of planes but saw only two of our own sea-planes. Just as we got the cattle out of the byre I spied nineteen weird-looking objects, which we afterwards knew to be anti-aircraft shells, over Kirkwall.

7 Sept. Nobody seems to know the rights of yesterday's air raid. Astley had a phone-message from the Post Office saying there were nine German planes over Kirkwall Harbour. Kirkwall people, here at a funeral, denied it and said it must have been our own planes. But Miss Balfour at the Castle had word that they were Germans ...

8 Sept. Everything very quiet – the peace before the storm? I'm afraid Hitler is plotting something. Britain has caught two German ships and taken them into Kirkwall. They put both crews on to one ship and sank the other. Three Germans somehow got away in a motor boat, and spent the night in the bay of Sandgarth. Tommy Nicolson saw them and reported it. Tom Sinclair and Bill Nicolson (both First War veterans) gave chase in Bill Nicolson's boat. A tug came from Kirkwall with armed men on it, touched here and set off too. The village people went into a 'steer' because the Germans were said to be armed and Bill and Tom weren't. They caught them, near Stronsay; found them unresisting and friendly; gave them cigarettes and were about to

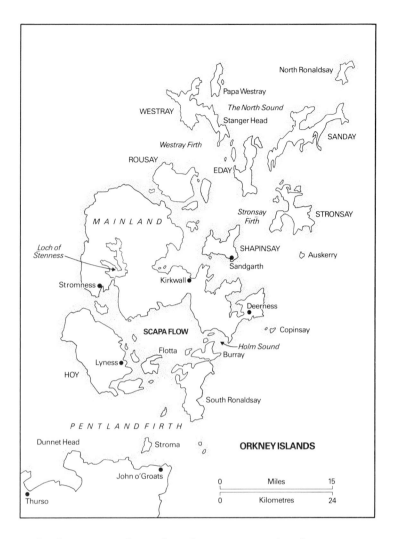

On the map:

North Ronaldsay
Papa Westray
WESTRAY
The North Sound
Stanger Head
SANDAY
Westray Firth
ROUSAY
EDAY
Stronsay Firth
STRONSAY
M A I N L A N D
Loch of Stenness
SHAPINSAY
Auskerry
Sandgarth
Kirkwall
Stromness
Deerness
Copinsay
SCAPA FLOW
Flotta
Holm Sound
Burray
Lyness
HOY
South Ronaldsay
P E N T L A N D   F I R T H
Dunnet Head
Stroma
ORKNEY ISLANDS
John o'Groats
Thurso

0	Miles	15
0	Kilometres	24

make them a pot of tea when the tug appeared and unceremoniously ordered the Germans aboard at gunpoint.

10 Oct. There is too little doing for my peace of mind! Hitler says he wants peace, but Britain won't give him peace, not on his terms! He is threatening to bomb every civilian town in Britain, sink every ship, and win the war! But he is NOT GOING to win. He is sure to try to bomb Kirkwall; Orkney is a dangerous place to live in. The King was in Scapa Flow and Kirkwall last week; Churchill the week before. There are rumours that Churchill said Orkney was not half-fortified – with the result that we are to have more coastal guns – one on this island too.

The summer is away and I don't know where it went. I enjoyed that summer, but I don't expect I'll enjoy another for a while. I *have* enjoyed it – the concert dance, the football dance, the Bible Class trip to Stromness ... I have a strange unrest tonight. It's raining and blowing all it can. Oh, if I could only wander, to far-away places! This wind gives me unrest. Ruby is going to be parlour-maid at the Castle.

I don't envy the Territorials on Stanger Head, this weather.

14 Oct.   Two air raids over Kirkwall while I was in town. The *Royal Oak* was blown up in Scapa Flow and about 800 lives lost – many young boys in training.

14 Nov.   There is a report that German planes were over Shetland again yesterday and dropped bombs. There is also a rumour that a spy was captured on Flotta, who had been poisoning the water supply. As there has been sickness among the troops, this is not impossible . . .

The siren sounded half an hour ago. Howe's flag is up; only it's not a flag, but a square sack of chaff!

There had been three Germans, adrift in an open boat, here in Orkney, trying to get back to Germany; they had apparently escaped from this area. They were caught near Fife, where the wind had blown them, exhausted, having gone without food for several days. The Chief Constable came out to the Castle and told Miss Balfour that they might land here – another false alarm.

20 Nov.   Germans were expected last night, as there had been a North Sea battle. I'm sure I heard Germans this morning when the siren went. The clack-clack-clack of their engines is distinctly different from the steady drone of our planes.

I ordered shoes from Kirkwall; the shop sent three pairs on approval. I kept a plain black lacing pair, although I didn't like them. There was a brown pair, rather fancy, price 7*s*., but Daddy says such cheap leather is no earthly use.

22 Nov.   Clack-clack-clack-brrr-clack!

'German!' we said, and ran out with the binoculars. It was a broad-winged monoplane, with tapering body and wide tail. When it came nearer I saw a cross on the wings – a black cross in a blue circle – with a white or yellow circle outside that. It clacked away southwards, then came back again, not very high, and circled right over us. Then it came lower, rose again, and faded into the clouds towards Kirkwall. As no warning was sounded, we wondered if it could be one of our planes after all, though it looked 'uncan' and we went in to study the flag-book to make sure.

Rumble, rumble! Bang-bang! The clacking engine was coming nearer, over Kirkwall. The guns from Holm and Kirkwall opened fire. The siren wailed, and I think I heard machine-gun fire. The clacking engine stopped momentarily and we thought they'd got it, but it started again, more loudly. A destroyer came round

Black Saturday: 14 October 1939. On that infamous day a surprise U-boat attack sank the 29,000 ton Royal Oak, *one of the country's mightiest battleships – 809 men went down with the ship in Scapa Flow.*

Harcosness, stopped, turned, and went out again. More shell-fire, then off went the plane into the S S E and we heard it no more. The 'Raiders Past' has not yet sounded. Probably they are too dumbfounded. The thing has foxed them this morning, by coming much lower than the Germans usually do.

Rumour has it that a U-boat was seen in Mell Bay the other night.

27 Nov. Severe westerly gale yesterday. The sea reeked through the reef, and right out through the String past Harcosness, like white smoke. I went down to the shore early in the morning and again in the afternoon, and found a good box, some oddments, and a small plank.

There are no poles left on Wideford Hill now, and only three and three-quarters on Holm. They were there yesterday afternoon, so they must have gone down in the night; they are said to be listening-posts for planes . . .

3 Dec. The Germans are not all bad. A U-boat sank a British ship and the crew took to the boats. The submarine came up and stood by. Some of the British were soaked and shivering, and the Germans served up hot food and drinks to them, and waited till a British vessel arrived to pick up survivors. Then the U-boat commander shouted 'Tell Churchill that there's some humanity!'

Girl, aged sixteen

1939   IN THE ARMY

It was a freezing cold night in December when we, a mortar company of the 1st Battalion of the Manchester Regiment, pulled into a small village. Our billet was the village hall. It was a change to sleep on a floor instead of slit-trenches. Next morning, after a wash at the pump, frozen solid, but soon running with some petrol over it, we were sitting around having our breakfast of tinned bacon and very hard biscuits when one of the lads asked what day it was. Every day seemed the same to us. However, after a lot of argument we asked an officer what day it was, and he had to work it out. It was Christmas Day 1939.

Boy, aged eighteen, France

JAN 1940   THE YOUNG COMMUNIST

I am having some difficulty in writing this letter as the guns are going off all round. At each explosion the windows shake and everything vibrates. I am sitting in a window overlooking the sea; it is a brilliant sunny day, it does not seem possible that somewhere, quite near, enemy planes are attempting to enter over the land. A few planes often enter the Channel on sunny days, but we have had no air raids here yet.

Once a German plane flew right above our hotel – anti-aircraft guns opened fire and we could see the shells bursting all round. The plane escaped over the Channel – somehow we were all glad when we saw that it had escaped; we dreaded seeing it crash into the sea. We did see the Norwegian ship [neutral] that was mined opposite here, burst into flames and sink. It was a terrible sight.

As far as I can see, the working class of England are not enthusiastic about this war. The government are issuing their propaganda frantically; everywhere there are posters – 'Freedom is in peril, defend it with all your might!' and 'Your courage, your cheerfulness, your resolution will bring us victory!', etc.

The dance-bands play patriotic songs over the radio all day, but the people are not impressed. They are dissatisfied with the falling wages and higher prices and with ever-growing conscription.

Yesterday at the cinema the organist played 'There'll always be an England' and asked the audience to join in. A few voices started but died away after the first bars. The audience merely looked bored.

In August I joined the Young Communist League, which is part of the Communist Party. There is no YCL here in Folkestone but I still keep in touch with the Lewisham Party. The secretary sends me all the papers and leaflets. There are no political meetings held here but on Sundays I go to Spiritualist Meetings which are quite interesting; though as far as I can see, Spiritualism is all faked.

I spend my evenings writing to school friends and other friends, about the war, the causes of war and what we must do for peace. I sometimes get the rudest letters in reply, but some of the girls show an interest and I feel that some of them are seeing events more clearly now. I expect you know that the Communist Party is advocating 'peace now'. Our YCL at home hold a meeting practically every night.

Girl, aged sixteen, Kent

1940   'WHAT IF HITLER WINS? HE *CAN'T*!'

22 Jan.   I hear that the Kirkwall schoolkids are to be evacuated to the Highlands. There is also a wild report that all the women and children in Orkney are to be evacuated, but this I do not believe.

23 Jan.   Went to the Guild meeting last night. We're having a bring and buy sale on 21 Feb.; each member brings a friend. I heard at the Guild that Kirkwall, Stromness and Flotta children *at least* are to be evacuated to Caithness and Sutherland. Some say all Orcadians will get orders to take up their beds and walk! I wouldn't mind going a bit further afield, but not on someone else's orders!

That smelly tanker that is sinking in Inganess Bay had been torpedoed after all. They have got the torpedo in Kirkwall – so much for their 'internal explosion'.

This is a lovely day – a lot of snow on the ground, hardly any wind, clear and sunny. On heavenly days like this one can't realize that there is a war.

27 Jan.   The evacuation scare was all tommy-rot! Such a scheme has never been mentioned! The *Orcadian* newspaper officially denied that any such thing had ever been spoken of.

Now we are to be livened up! Two A A guns are coming to Shapinsay, and 100 men with two officers.

Wednesday was to have been our Burns' supper, but it was postponed until next Monday. The snow is all away. Oh, it's cold!

31 Jan. There was a dance last night. Some of our Territorials were coming home from Flotta, but because of bad weather they couldn't get home. The dance went on without them. We had quite a good evening.

I have found a lot of wood on the shore lately. Three ships have been sunk near here; two destroyers somewhere between Copinsay and Auskerry, and a patrol boat at Deerness. Very few lives saved. Jock Irving found a body near Sandgarth.

An anti-aircraft gun is to be put at Stromberry, and a searchlight. A 'heavy' is to be put at the Galt.

5 Feb. Three bodies have come ashore here, two in Sands and one near Hillside. Finding the bodies has rather scared the Sands people. Bill Nicolson [coastguard], going past the place where the bodies had lain, one dark night, nearly jumped sky-high when something gripped his trouser-leg! It was only a wee white dog!

A German plane came over on Saturday morning. It bombed the *Rota* but didn't hurt her; then off the east side of Shapinsay it machine-gunned an armed trawler. The trawler was not damaged but one man had bullets in his arm. The plane circled for a time then went off. Our patrols got up in full force after it was away. They said on the wireless this morning that three of our bombers chased if off! Utter nonsense! It went off at its own leisure. Not only the Germans tell fibs, it appears!

Only John Kirkness and I turned up for Bible Class this evening. Rev. J. Alan Robertson took us into the Manse for supper, and it was past ten before I got home. Daddy was just about to come and look for me. I wish he wouldn't get the wind up every time I'm late – it's so horribly silly.

10 Feb. Found a keg of Danish butter yesterday at Steiro – quite good, though a bit dirty on the outside, and the keg will fall to pieces if it gets too much handling. Seawater ran out when I hauled it up. It weighs 100lb. Reckoning it at 1*s.* a pound, it's worth £5. I'm going to report it. I also found an empty cask at the noust, in excellent condition.

Germany lost two U-boats yesterday.

22 Feb. Reported my butter and got a form to fill in. The butter is in Kirkwall now, and I'll get salvage according to what it sells for.

A destroyer was lost off Westray, on Sunday I think. She was one of a convoy.

16 Mar. Why did the Minister invite me to dance Strip-the-willow? I got into such a mix-up! I'm still sleepy after the dance.

Evening Another visit from Jerry! What an evening! I was up at Astley shop when Jim Stewart shouted 'Come out and see the firing!'

We all ran out, but thought it was a practice till Jim said 'I hear Germans!' It looked like fireworks and was really lovely. Gigantic sparklers going up, and great flashes from the Fleet in the Flow. About a dozen planes overhead, all lighted up, and making a noise like nothing holy. There was machine-gun fire coming down, and shells bursting above us. Suddenly a great fire burst out near Kirkwall, and we all yelled 'The oil tanks! The aerodrome!' But it went out again suddenly. I'm sure it was a ship.

More fire came down, just at the Holm searchlights. A lull, then nine planes with lights on went hell for leather northwards. Just as I was leaving, they got an air-raid warning! As I stepped outside I counted eight planes in the north and a roar of Germans in the distance. Very little firing, just a shot at a time, as I made for home. When I reached Newhouse it started again, fiercer than ever. Sixteen searchlights on. A great flash from Stromness, lighting up the west Mainland hills brilliantly. Shells burst right overhead, more firing seemed directly beside me. I was nearly gassed with gunpowder; the whole place reeked of it. Planes roaring overhead; the firing fiercer than ever. Did I run? The shells were right above me and the flashes at my very nose. Shrapnel falling, so I went hell for leather too!

There wasn't much firing after I got home. Honestly, I was not frightened, but I was excited, and I'm always chasing after excitement. All quiet now, the planes are down and the searchlights off. We'll have rain tomorrow . . .

17 Mar. The Germans hit a battleship last night, and killed seven on board her. She was only damaged. We got one German plane; it went off, blazing. Seven cottages in Stenness were hit, seven civilians injured and one killed. The Bridge of Waithe is blown up.

Lord Haw-Haw says they have accomplished what they wanted to do in Orkney and all their planes came safely home. He said some time ago they were going to bomb Orkney on 15 March. He was only one day out.

Jim says there are a number of the Fleet in Scapa, plus a good many 'dummies'.

There was a lot of confusion during the raid. The pilots who went up were young, practically untrained men, the rumour runs. Also we heard the guns were not quite quick enough off the mark. At Holm an officer phoned to the guns: 'There's a squadron of Germans overhead – open fire!' The planes were out of range before they fired ...

There are ten Territorials here on Shapinsay, preparing for a big squad that comes next week. Two went past here yesterday and waved to me; I waved back.

22 Mar.   The last convoy that went out past here was attacked off the east coast by eight Germans. Three ships were damaged, one had to be abandoned.

Forty Territorials were to have arrived here yesterday; don't know if they have come or not, but I'll find out when I go to the village for provisions. Our dress-rehearsal for the concert went not too badly. John Kirkness won't speak out properly – says that's because he has to have a 'lady's voice' (six feet tall and pretending to be a girl indeed!). Aggie has measles, so Lydia has to take her place in the duet with Barry.

The Territorials are coming to the dance!

The rain seems eternal – very mild soft rain, but naturally it wets you! Jean Gray has been in Stromness and says she saw the bombed cottages, and the Bridge of Waithe isn't demolished, only damaged. Some people in Birsay never knew the raid was on.

23 Mar.   The concert went off OK, far better than the rehearsal. Our sketch wasn't bad. People say my recitation was good.

25 Mar.   The Territorials have got their searchlight in Elwick-bank Park. I believe the big thing they took into the Fort is a gun after all. Their enormous lorry got through the iron gate without knocking the pillars down! The lorry went past here a little while ago with men and a big trailer behind. The men were singing and they all waved. Mother lectured me for waving back, and when they returned she wouldn't let me go out in case I waved to them again! The men are planning to have a dance on Wednesday night, but I won't be allowed to go.

27 Mar.   The 'thing' at the Fort is a generator after all, and the searchlight quite a small apparatus. The other large object is a new kind of detector – the very latest device.

We hear Miss Balfour is making the private soldiers billeted with her eat their food outside in the cold. She even refused to let them put their cooking stoves in the yard outside the kitchen door – the stoves are in the tennis court, and the men must eat there in the rain! And the lieutenant is treated like a gentleman, while he would prefer to be out with his men. They must take their boots off before coming indoors . . .

There's a rumour we are to have fifty Gordons, with guns. The Lancashire men are nice, though we have difficulty in understanding their speech, and they have the same difficulty with us, unless we speak English. (I don't like the Orcadian dialect anyhow.)

Evening Rattle-bang. 'It's Jerry! Come out and see the fire-works!' Twilight was beginning. Tracer bullets climbed upwards. A pale searchlight appeared over Kirkwall. Searchlight beams were all around, from Liviness, Cot-on-Hill, Stromberry and a lot from Holm and the south-west. Then everything as silent as the grave.

Suddenly, firing again, and a big display lit up the world. It was magnificent, beautiful. Our Shapinsay searchlights swept the sky, and Mainland was alive with sweeping lights and twinkling bullets and shells, and flashes of big guns to the south. I stood yelling encouragement at our searchlight batteries. I counted thirty-seven searchlights up at one time. Then the noise died away, and a voice from Liviness called through a megaphone 'Out!' The light shut off. I marched around for some time, whistling 'Run, rabbit, run' not very tunefully, I'm afraid, for I was a bit excited. Every raid we get, I long to be at the guns! These raids seem to rouse the Viking in me.

Jim Stewart says the whole German fleet is out – 100 or more. Norway is not objecting to our mining her waters. It's all a bit confusing . . .

9 April. Two German planes brought down last night – another won't get home.

America reports that Germany has invaded Denmark, and that German soldiers are parading in Danish towns. Norway is at war with Germany over Britain mining their waters. The 100 German ships are mainly armed trawlers, minesweepers and a few battleships, and they are heading for Norway.

About 8.30 Uncle Andrew came in. 'You'll hear something in a little while,' he prophesied. The siren wailed just as he spoke. A great noise of our planes rising . . . shells burst in an enormous barrage – a great black line in the sky. Great flashes from Lyness – whole batteries opening up at once. Our lighted planes scoured about, high above the shell barrage. As it grew darker, the firing increased.

'Look, a German machine-gunning!' An enemy plane, going like smoke, was rat-tatting with his tail-gun, over Kirkwall. A shell crashed right behind him. He went off, then. Suddenly, the west side searchlight swept across the sky – and in the beam was an enormous plane! A great bomber, flying for its life, so low that one could easily have hit it with a shotgun! Four great engines under the wings; and red fire shooting down from the tail-gun, right between Hannatoft and the Old Manse. We lost sight of it then. Our four Shapinsay searchlights met and crossed overhead. An armed trawler, in the bay below us, fired. A faint red light appeared at the aerodrome. A pom-pom went crack, crack. We heard the men on the Elwickbank light shouting. The officer's car went past again. More bullets, flashes, searchlights. The lapwings were crying, and above it all a pale crescent moon looked down. It was weirdly beautiful.

10 May Norway is almost gone – and Germany has invaded Holland and Belgium simultaneously, dropping hundreds of men by parachute. We still have Narvik, but that's all of Norway.

There have been great ructions in Parliament, Churchill versus Chamberlain. They think Chamberlain is too slack and we must adopt some of Germany's tactics, or we'll never win the war. There was a vote. Chamberlain is still Prime Minister, but Churchill has almost supreme power now.

15 May Jim Hayworth [searchlight battery] came here last evening and said there was a submarine in here in the bay last night at two o'clock! A searchlight crew in Tankerness spied it cruising unconcernedly on the surface. They phoned Kirkwall, and all the men got orders to stand to. 'L' section from Liviness came out, watched for a minute, then went to bed again. There's a scare on that German parachutists may try to make a landing on Orkney. There were planes with parachutists on their way here on Sunday but our fighters drove them off. All the soldiers are to have more rifles, and four men are to be on guard together at night.

20 May The war gets more serious. Holland gave in last week. The Germans are half-way through Belgium, and this is one of the decisive battles of the war. 'L' section got orders to leave on Saturday; word came in the morning to pack up and be away by one o'clock. I hear heavy firing in the east, but cannot see anything.

21 May All last night I dreamed of quarries and water – very vivid dreams. This morning a case of suicide or accidental drowning occurred in Sands.

There was a great deal of firing last night – the Holm battery made a mistake – fired sixteen rounds with a twelve-pounder at a British ship and sent her to the bottom. The Germans have broken through the French lines and are some way in through France. Last night the news was bad – they had captured Arras.

25 May The Germans are right through the French lines now – they've reached Boulogne. I didn't hear the nine o'clock news last night but the news is getting worse and worse. What if Hitler wins? He *can't*. In all human reason he can't.

Girl, aged sixteen

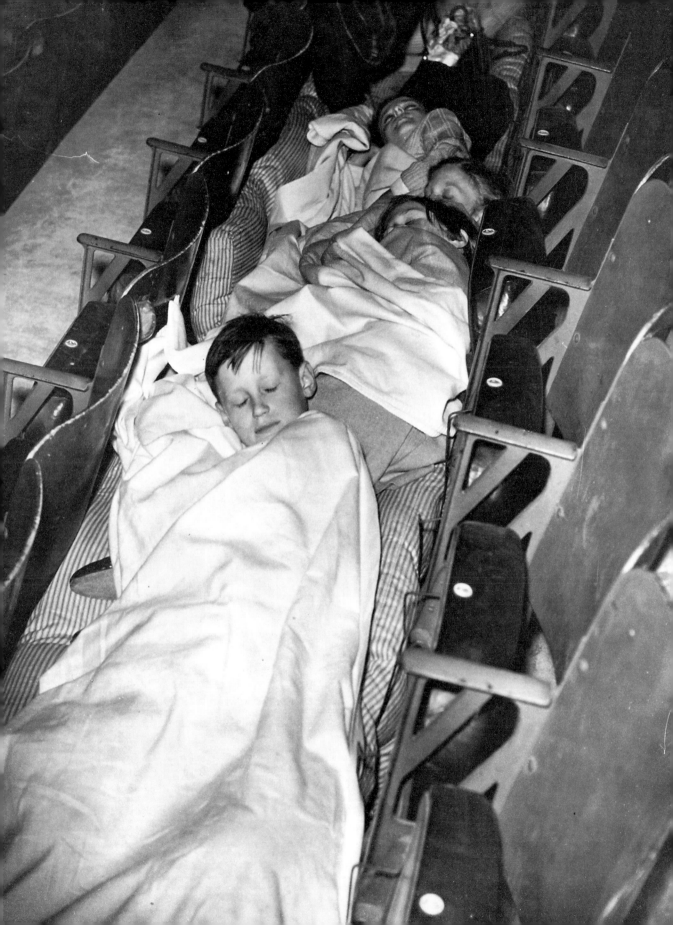

CHAPTER 5 THE FALL OF HOLLAND AND FRANCE

MAY 1940 HOLLAND

I remember the day the Germans invaded Holland. The Dutch people fought very hard, and were very sure they would defeat the evil Germans. But as the Dutch armies saw their soldiers killed in great numbers, soon they had to admit defeat. The reason that so many were killed was because when the soldiers opened crates of what was supposed to be ammunition, they contained sand and gravel. Placed there by persons employed by the Germans before the Invasion ... The Germans bombed Rotterdam and razed this great city to the ground. This would happen to a large town every day, declared the Germans, until the Dutch people capitulated. The feeling of pain and hopelessness I will never forget.

I remember the dreadful rules made by the German dictators. The noise of the dreaded jackboots as they marched through the towns. The identity cards we had to carry. First just little cards, but later we had to have our fingerprint on our card, as so many people were carrying false papers.

I remember listening to the BBC, risking our lives, as this was punishable by death. At night the hidden radio was brought out and all members of the household would congregate for the news. One member had to watch and listen in the front room, in case any German guards were snooping about.

I remember the look on the faces of the Jews. At first they were demoted from their jobs. Most held very high jobs at Philips. They could only hold the lowest jobs, by decree of the Germans. So they had to clean toilets, often in the same works where they had held high positions before the war. Shops, buses, cafés and cinemas were all *verboten* to the Jews. They were not allowed

Dutch and Belgian refugee children, evacuated from the invaded and stricken Low Countries by boat, sleep on mattresses in the Empress Stadium, Earls Court, London.

73

cars or bikes and had to walk everywhere. After a while they had to wear large yellow stars of David on all their clothing and it was pitiful to see their faces grow more frightened and worn as the war progressed. After three years they disappeared from the town, either sent to the gas chamber or gone into hiding.

I remember the Germans stealing all the food, so there wasn't enough in the shops, and enforcing strict rationing. The rations were not enough to keep a mouse alive, and at first trade on the black market was rife. Then, as food became unobtainable, the ingenuity of my mother became apparent. Coffee-substitute was made from roasted ground barley with a bit of chicory powder for colouring. Roasted and ground tulip bulbs were used for coffee too. For cornflour a large potato was sliced and left in some water, and the floury substance which accumulated in the bottom of the bowl was used as starch or thickening for broth. Potatoes for breakfast was a luxury and most days breakfast was missed out altogether. Mothers would stand for hours in a queue with a bowl for some kohlrabi. Neither potatoes nor kohlrabi were peeled before boiling, and often the string which had tied the bunches of kohlrabi was also cooked for good measure. The smell of this hash was unbelievable, but it was warm and stopped the hunger pangs. Hunger is a pain, that gnaws at your stomach and just will not go away. No matter how many cups of water one drank to fill that aching stomach, that dreadful feeling would not go away.

When at night the sirens sounded, because British planes were crossing Holland on their missions to Germany, we would sit in our little air-raid shelter, and while waiting for the 'all clear' our stomachs would rumble for food. My sister's favourite saying was 'Oh, I would love a bacon sandwich'. This would make our mouths water, and going to sleep was almost impossible.

I remember the Resistance was very strong in Eindhoven. One day they blew up an ammunition train. The Germans were livid. They went to the Philips factory and took twenty men from their work. The poor men were put against an air-raid shelter in town and shot. A curfew was announced and everyone had to be indoors by seven o'clock. The next day some flowers were placed on the spot where the twenty men were shot, and again the Germans took another twenty men and repeated the same dreadful act.

I remember all young Dutch men were called up for working in German ammunition factories. These were regularly bombed by our friends the British, so the Germans would not risk the lives of their own people. My brother was called up to work in Germany, but with the help of a Resistance worker a very clever

April 1940. Still-neutral Holland declares a state of siege. Almost certainly a 'posed' photograph, and yet the tension in the people is real. Their world hangs on the brink of dreadful change, all the more awful because they stayed neutral in 'the last lot'. This is how we felt, 3 September 1939.

plan was devised. My brother reported to the station as ordered. When his official papers were in the hands of the German guards, he was spirited away by the Resistance, and given false identity cards and returned home.

His absence was not discovered till the train arrived at the Ruhr. Soon the Germans were knocking at our front door, rifles at the ready.

Mother was also ready, even to be shot for the sake of her son, and was as rude as possible to the Germans. My sister was in bed suffering from flu. As the soldiers started searching at the top of the house, Mother waited until they approached my sister's bedroom. When they opened the bedroom door, Mother exclaimed in a loud voice that she suffered from tuberculosis, which was dreaded in the war. Many died from it, and the Germans were terrified of it. Without further ado, the search was abandoned, and my brother was safe, hiding in the rafters of the little stable behind our house.

I remember the cold winter of 1943. No coal was available and the house was freezing. Mother (as only mothers would) proclaimed she was quite warm during the day. But something had to be done to stop her catching pneumonia. So my brother, sister and I decided to chop down a tree in the wood near by, between the town and the airfield. In the wood was a camouflaged German Military Hospital, so we had to be careful. We took axes and saws and an old bike without tyres for transporting our spoils. After curfew, when it was quite dark we crept to the woods, past the guards on duty at the 'Krankenrivier' and deep into the trees. It was hard work, and the fear of detection made us shudder with fright every time we heard an unusual noise.

We laid the trunk of the tree across the dilapidated bike and were nearly home when my sister, who was carrying the axes, was stopped by the police. Thank God it was a Dutch policeman, who lived near and knew our family. He confiscated the axes and called on Mother the next day, warning her not to let us out after curfew, as the Germans would not hesitate to shoot us.

I remember food becoming so scarce, that one Christmas we ate a stray cat for dinner, pretending it was rabbit. Not the Spirit of Christmas, but we had nothing else . . .

Girl, aged fifteen, Eindhoven

The greatest cartoon of the war. I always had the feeling that David Low was actually a personal friend of Winnie's, and possibly a member of the Government. Only Churchill excelled him in capturing our moods. He probably did more to win the war than the whole Ministry of Information. I had this picture on my bedroom wall.

" VERY WELL, ALONE "

We lads had two kings in the war. We had a reverence for King George VI – brave, loving, suffering, stammering. He really felt for the bomb-victims he talked to. I think we would have died defending him, but we never thought he could win the war for us.

Churchill – big Winnie – was the lad for us. We all wished we could be Winnie. What our gang-leader did for our gang, Winnie did for Britain. It was the marvellous way he insulted the enemy gang leaders.

Winnie appeared in the comic strips too (though King George VI never did) always smiling, two fingers up, entirely in control. He frequently colluded with ever-victorious comic-strip heroes like 'Big Eggo', 'Desperate Dan' and 'Lord Snooty'.

We saw him not as a great, distant war leader, but as a naughty, irrepressible super-child who could do anything. The tommy-gun pose (ironically, from a German propaganda leaflet) is typical – he looks so like a child pleased with himself – and the formal suit and hat is half the joke. But we knew it wasn't just a pose with the gun – he would really fire it, and score a bullseye, without bothering to take the hat off his head, or the inevitable cigar from his mouth. And he dared wear funny clothes, like his famous siren-suit. He invariably gave the impression he was not only going to win, but was actually enjoying every minute of it. When he passed among us, people would shout, 'Give the bastards one for us, Winnie', and he would lift his hat and smile obligingly.

1940 THE FALL OF FRANCE

There was a sort of tingle in the air when I got up that morning; a sinking feeling in the gut, if you thought too much about it, and yet a heady excitement as well. Our radio was on all day, and they kept playing a fierce trumpet record, called 'Trumpet Voluntary', between the announcements. Whoever thought of that was a genius; it keyed you up. I'd never realized why armies used trumpets before. It was harsh and bitter, and made you feel braver.

I couldn't understand why the French had surrendered. According to my war-map, they still had nine-tenths of their country left. In the Last Lot, the Germans had nearly got to Paris, had bombarded Paris with bloody huge guns like Big Bertha, and the French hadn't given in, and won in the end. What was the *matter* with them?

Of course, they had old-fashioned weapons. Daft old-fashioned helmets with a ridge along the top, and pale blue uniforms and puttees same as in the last war, instead of our new battledress. Their bombers tended to have three engines, and their fighters were always ten miles slower than ours, and their tanks had absurd round turrets and their submarines had huge guns instead of sensible torpedoes. But that was no reason for giving *up*.

I went for a walk, I was so worried. Met a kid on a building-site who said the French had only *pretended* to surrender; they'd waved a white flag, and when the Germans got out of their trenches, the French had shot them down like dogs . . . this was the first sensible suggestion I'd heard all day. I ran home to tell Dad the good news; he was not impressed.

People kept saying the French were *decadent*. Hints of black underwear and too much ooh-la-la in Paris. Till somebody said not in front of the child. My mother thought that lack of decent flush-toilets had sapped their morale. They drank wine instead of tea, *every day*! My father was pretty quiet. He said the French had stood up to Jerry pretty well in the Last Lot. Then Mr Churchill broadcast and said 'The Battle of France is over; the Battle of Britain is about to begin.'

I felt better, and went out on my bike to look for signs of the Battle of Britain.

Boy, aged ten, Tyneside

78

This magical Low cartoon marked the formation of an all-party war cabinet – hardly a very exciting occasion for a working-class boy.

The awesome thing is the rolling-up of sleeves. Working men really did roll up their sleeves in 1940, very slowly and methodically, almost meditatively, before starting a job or a fight. You spat on the palms of your hands, too; surely a remnant of the old magic.

But here, glory be, it's not just socialist Morrison and docker Bevin ... but near-aristocrats and gentle-men like Anthony Eden. They had grasped reality at last, and joined us workers. And behind, the endless trailing line of all of us – including me and my dad, rolling our sleeves up too. In this cartoon are the seeds not only of Churchill's 1945 victory, but also of his 1945 defeat, at the hands of the Labour Party. Anthony Eden was much admired by working men, for his pre-war anti-appeasement re-signation. But he was admired even more by working-class women – he shared 'star quality' with the British Hollywood greats Ronald Colman and Douglas Fairbanks Jr., whom he rather resembled.

Chamberlain Greenwood Halifax   Sinclair Duff Cooper Alexander Eden   K. Wood
Churchill   Attlee   Bevin   Morrison   Amery

CHAPTER 6 SHELTERS, GASMASKS AND BARRAGE BALLOONS

1939 ANDERSON SHELTER

The government didn't *build* shelters for you. Council workmen just came with a lorry and dumped the bits on your front lawn and left you to get on with it. We didn't think much of the bits, lying out in the rain, gathering rainwater. Just thin bits of corrugated iron, like some old shed. People felt they'd be safer in their houses, solid bricks and mortar. They weren't going out in the middle of the night to bury themselves in a *grave*.

Then my father saw an Anderson that had received a direct hit; he said there was quite a lot of it left; the house it had belonged to was just a heap of bricks.

So he and our neighbour Frank Spedding got cracking. They put me in charge of sorting and counting the bits and pieces, while they dug, but I soon got down into the hole. It had vertical sides, like a grave. Bits of worm kept poking out, then the worm would fall out altogether. It all smelt *good*, like gardening. People were calling out to each other, from hole to hole, and handing round tea. I got my pistol, and dreamt I was in the Trenches, in the Last Lot, and just about to lead my men Over the Top against the Germans, who were dug-in in Delaval Avenue. We found old clay pipes and blackened pennies, but only from 1935. Dad said he must have had a hole in his pocket, gardening.

Two foot six down, we came across an earthenware pipe running right across the hole. Mr Spedding, who was a builder, said it was a field-drain, from the time when our houses were fields. If we dug down through it, all the water in the field when it rained would end up in our shelter. So they decided to stop digging.

Mr Spedding, being a builder, got all sorts of bits and pieces, and we made that shelter a real home from home. The floor was made of old maroon front doors, bought for a bob. The inside walls were painted white, and Mr Spedding threw handfuls of little bits of cork at the wet paint, so they stuck on; he said this would absorb the moisture from our breath, so condensation wouldn't run down the walls in winter. (Later, picking those bits of cork off the walls stopped me screaming while the bombs were dropping.) Mr Spedding also 'acquired' a lot of sandbags from somewhere, and soaked them in creosote, to stop the wet earth rotting them. I got really hooked on creosote, which I'd never smelt before; kept on going back to sniff them. We made them into a fine wall, all round the shelter, to keep the earth from falling off it. We also used them to make a porch, to keep rain off the shelter door. By the time we put the stout wood door on, and Mr Spedding had run electric cable out from the house, we

All the family helped: Anderson shelters going up . . .

. . . and coming down. It is possible a family survived in this shelter . . .

82

were as snug as a bug in a rug. Electric light, electric fire, and we used to sit in armchairs making toast. Dad would have liked a picture on the wall, but all the walls were curved.

Then the man came from the council. Nothing was right for him: we couldn't have a wooden door on the shelter; a bomb would turn it into a mass of splinters, and drive them through our flesh as we sat there. We could only have an old blanket over the door. We couldn't have electric light, as the bomb might cut the cable and fry us alive, if the cable touched the metal walls. Worst of all, the shelter should be three feet deep, not two feet six.

Dad told him about the field-drain. Dad said he wanted a shelter, not a well for watering the roses. But the man kept on waving his little steel ruler, and saying if we didn't put it three feet down, the council would come and take the shelter away, and we could do without.

We put it down three feet; I don't think Dad stopped swearing from start to finish. Slowly, the shelter filled up with water like a swimming-pool. We did water the roses from it. We spent the winter raids sheltering in the cupboard under the stairs.

Boy, aged nine, Tyneside

1939 A VERY EARLY AGE

I was still in my pram when the war started. I remember the siren going and my mam coming to pick me up. She carried me downstairs; my dad followed everyone else. He was very small as he was a jockey. He tripped on the third-bottom stair. He ended up wedged inside my pram and we had to push him in it, out to the air-raid shelter.

In the shelter I remember it being very quiet and I was lying in my pram with my mam holding my hand. Everyone was scared stiff.

Boy, Liverpool

. . . They certainly survived in this one. The bomb, falling deeply into soft soil, has sent most of its blast harmlessly upwards . . . hence slates are intact on nearby roofs. Note the essential thumbs-up sign — solely used for the benefit of newspaper photographers.

1939 SHELTERS

Our friends and neighbours were digging up their gardens to instal Anderson shelters, but not us. My father had a curious attitude towards air raids. What seemed to worry him more than anything else was flying glass splinters. Either he was an optimist, who thought our house would never receive a direct hit, or else a pessimist, who believed that if we did we'd be dead anyway. He preferred to convert our coalhouse into an air-raid shelter, by the simple process of having the external door bricked-up, and a hole broken through into the scullery. (Another small store was built on to the back of the house to contain the coal.) When the sirens sounded we crawled into the coalhouse and sat there, well away from any windows, but under a slate roof right against the outside wall.

Perhaps someone pointed out the dangers because, after a while, we stopped using the 'shelter'. During one particularly bad raid we took a mattress downstairs and slept on the lounge floor. This led to a grand reorganization of furniture in the house. My parents' bedroom became an upstairs lounge, and the lounge became a family bedroom, with the wardrobe placed across the french windows to shield us from the glass.

Boy, aged ten, London

1939 GASMASK

One annoyance was the gasmask in its clumsy cylindrical metal case. You had to carry it with you all the time, and the case bumped against your side most uncomfortably when you walked.

Although I could breathe in it, I felt as if I couldn't. It didn't seem possible that enough air was coming through the filter. The covering over my face, the cloudy perspex in front of my eyes, and the overpowering smell of rubber, made me feel slightly panicky, though I still laughed each time I breathed out, and the edges of the mask blew a gentle raspberry against my cheeks.

Boy, aged ten, London

Hitler will send no warning –

so always carry your gas mask

The nearest we ever got to hysteria was about gasmasks, before the war had even started properly. Notice again what a boon 'Adolf' was to the Ministry of Home Security.

1939 'MAKE A GAME OF IT'

'Are your little ones used to seeing you in *your* mask? Make a game of it, calling it "Mummy's funny face" or something of the kind. Then if the time comes when you really have to wear it, you won't be a terrifying apparition to the child.'

Radio broadcast, 1939

Silly propaganda. An obviously posed photograph with the girls simply standing. Had they tried exercising, their masks would have steamed up immediately. There were even photographs of 'nudes' from the Windmill Theatre, wearing little but gasmasks.

1939 GAS PRACTICE

The one thing we were certain of was that the Germans would use poison gas. Babies had gasmasks; horses had gasmasks; both were the same size, except the whole baby went inside, but only the horse's head. The baby's mother had to pump air into it, through a concertina-thing on the side.

Young children had gay blue-and-red ones that looked like Mickey Mouse. Soldiers had very grand hideous ones, with round eyepieces and a long trunk like an elephant. Wardens' were similar, but without the trunk. Ours had a short trunk, and a large window for our eyes. The moment you put it on, the window misted up, blinding you. Our Mums were told to rub soap on the inside of the window, to prevent this. It made it harder to see than ever, and you got soap in your eyes.

There was a rubber washer under your chin, that flipped up and hit you, every time you breathed in. You breathed out with a farting noise round your ears. If you blew really hard, you could make a very loud farting noise indeed. (You got caned for doing that during gas practices.) The bottom of the mask soon filled up with spit, and your face got so hot and sweaty you could have *screamed*.

Once we had our masks tested; we were led through an air-raid shelter that the wardens had filled with tear-gas. Most of us noticed nothing, but Charlie Blower's mask didn't work. He just sat in class all morning with tears streaming down his face, then the teacher sent him home.

The cardboard boxes that gasmasks came in fell apart inside a week. Our Dads bought us long metal cylinders like the German soldiers carried their gasmasks in. We used to carry them round on dog-leads across our shoulders. We used gasmasks in fights, whirling them round our heads, swinging them like swords; they could cut your head open, if you didn't dodge. The guy with the most dented gasmask was the hero. We used to carry bottles of ink and sweets and secret treasures inside. When you had a sudden gas practice, this could be very embarrassing.

Boy, aged ten, Tyneside

1939 BARRAGE BALLOONS

Barrage balloons moved into the streets where I lived. We talked to the airmen and airwomen who operated them. The equipment consisted of a large wagon with a winch on the back. This was covered with a cage to protect the operators in case the hawser snapped and whipped back. During bad weather the balloons were brought back to the ground. On more than one occasion I saw balloons that had been cut free. This was done by chopping through the hawser with a sharp axe, in sudden cases of bad weather, or balloons being set on fire by lightning or by enemy planes shooting at them. It was very dangerous for people on the ground because the trailing hawser was sometimes dragged across the rooftops, knocking off chimneys and damaging roofs.

Boy, Liverpool

1939 A DEMENTED KITE

I got to know our local barrage balloon team very well. They were sited on the tennis courts just below our back garden and I spent many hours watching. We occasionally lost a balloon by its breaking free, when it would suddenly shoot up to a tremendous height before drifting away, no doubt to be used as a target for some marauding fighter plane. Alternatively, the ears or vanes would tear, and on these occasions the balloon would go out of control and behave like a demented kite. The crew would try and bring it in but it would tear round on the end of its wire, taking off chimney-pots and roofs. On one such occasion the wire crossed the trolley-bus cables and disabled all electric transport along the Plumstead road for hours.

Boy, London

Like herds of silver elephants, their fins rippling in every breeze ... They brought down few aircraft, but raised morale.

1940 FEELING SAFE

We had five barrage balloons, including one on a ship that went out into the middle of the river during raids. The Germans shot down one, the Fish Quay Buster. But it was replaced the next day, which made the Germans seem pretty pointless.

Sometimes the balloons flew low, sometimes high; no pattern to it. People used to discuss them, like they'd discussed weather in peacetime. 'I see the balloons are low tonight!' It must mean *something*.

Finally the mums decided they were a kind of barometer for air raids. If the balloons were low, a raid was expected. If they flew high, it was safe to let the kids out to play. The higher the balloons, the further we were allowed to roam.

One sunny night, we went off to the Coast Road bridge, about a mile, to watch for army convoys. My mate went fishing for newts. I lay on my back in the dry summer grass, and suddenly noticed the balloons. *Incredibly* high, the sunlight catching their silver sides, making them glint like stars. So many ... I felt incredibly safe; so many balloons, so high. I hadn't felt so safe since war started. Hitler couldn't possibly win.

I lay on, in a kind of dream, my mate splashing some yards off. The sun set, and still the sides of the myriad balloons glinted.

I called out 'Aren't the balloons like stars?'

'They aren't balloons, they *are* the stars!'

Suddenly, it was dark, and we were far too far from home.

We ran all the way.

Boy, aged ten, Tyneside

CHAPTER 7 DAYLIGHT RAIDS

18 AUG
1940 ATTACK ON KENLEY AIRFIELD

Eight-year-old Brian Crane had been playing football with some young friends when the sight of the large formation caught their attention. The children gazed up in awe at the armada passing overhead. Then, too late, the siren began to sound and bombs began to fall. Instant confusion; the horror-struck boys stood paralysed, not knowing what to do. Then a lady shouted 'Run home to your mummies, quick! They'll be worried!' And run the children did, as fast as their legs could carry them. 'The owner of the ball kept calling "You've left my bloody ball." We hadn't. I was clutching it firmly to my stomach, probably wishing it was my mother.' Half-crying to themselves, the children ran on, people shouting at them from all directions. 'Get off the street! Mind the shrapnel! Get home quick!' All of this intermingled with the crump of exploding bombs and the menacing drone of aircraft. Finally a concerned lady insisted that the boys take cover in her house. They were ushered into a cupboard under the stairs and plied with milk, biscuits and toffee. 'I sat with my knees under my chin, pressing the football into my chest and remembering every good thing my mother had ever done for me.'

From Alfred Price, The Hardest Day (*Scribner, 1980*).

1940 LIFE MUST GO ON

The Mission Bazaar is today and I am dressed up as a Red Indian. It is going to be jolly nice unless the Jerries want to pay a visit to us. The siren is a 'stale story' because it goes every night at

Quite a small bomb, really ... land-mines were much worse.

a quarter past seven. Is there any chance of you and Daddy getting a house yet? I suppose all this can be blamed on 'Funny Face Hitler'?

Girl, convent boarding school, Hampshire

LETTERS FROM A RAID

Dear Mummy,

Thankyou for your letter and I hope you got mine. It is really jolly nice here. Last night I moved (and Bee, but she went into another room) – moved into the rest-room [infirmary] not because I was ill, but because of bombs. You see we were on the top floor – only the roof on top of us. M. Horan is sleeping there too.

I go down to the farm nearby all the day ... The siern has just gone and we are in a shelter, ha, ha! The siern always goes when I am at the farm. We have had two more Raids in fact more I am sure. The 'All Clear' has just gone what a short Raid they passed but they were lots and lots of them. Oh dear! No more news.

Love, Jill

Dear Mummy and Daddy,

We had an exciting time on Thursday (us) You see we had an *Air Raid* warning in the night. It was funny, mistresses in dressing-gowns. Nuns half-dressed. (I still had my plate in my mouth ha, ha!) We were down in the shelter about an hour. We played games and went nearly to sleep. We said the Rosary too. The next day we were very tired so we had to rest. Most of the school went to sleep.

Jill

Girl, convent boarding school, Hampshire

1940 FERRY CROSS THE MERSEY

I had just got married when war broke out. I was living in Wallasey. One day my friend and myself took a shopping trip on the ferry to Liverpool. I was eight months pregnant. Our trip was quite successful and I had managed to purchase some baby clothes with coupons I had been carefully saving for months. We were on our way home and the ferry was halfway across,

Where were these East End kids going? What were they doing? Anything to get into the war.

Lifebuoy toilet soap's contribution to final victory. The boys look suspiciously eager to bath. We were far too busy, and our mothers would not have approved of bathing in public, in other people's hot water. Perhaps it happened in the South of England?

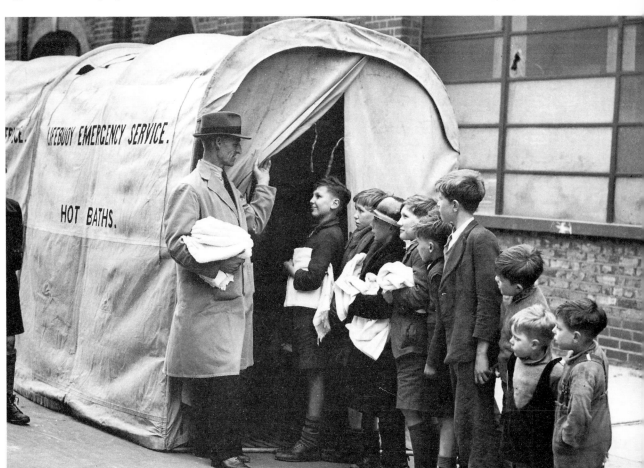

In our eyes the Stuka dive-bomber was the ultimate magic evil Nazi bird. Only J.R.R. Tolkien, with his Nazgul in Lord of the Rings, gets anywhere near their horror today. They were Hitler's personal demons. Like the Nazgul, they cast a shadow of terror; men's hearts failed when they appeared. On the newsreels, we had watched them destroy the terrified streams of refugees, and helpless soldiers of Spain, Poland, Holland, France. They flew in geometrically straight formations, and dived on their prey near-vertically, paralysing them with the built-in whistles on their wings, that wailed like banshees. With their queer cranked wings and fitted spatted undercarriage, we boys found them miracles of evil shapes, impossible to draw. But we impersonated them more often than Hitler or Churchill, cranking our arms wildly and screeching down steep hills to the consternation of old ladies.

At the beginning of the Battle of Britain, Stukas were sent to attack south-coast shipping and radar masts. They flew into a cloud of Spitfires and Hurricanes off Portland Bill, and were slaughtered. There was a radio commentator watching: I'll never forget his hysterical shouts of delight and relief as they started going down. 'Like shooting rats in a barrel', he kept saying, 'like shooting rats in a barrel'. In that magical moment, I knew that Hitler was going to lose the war. Now, when I read of the Nazgul falling in fiery ruin, at the end of Lord of the Rings, it's the Stukas I see.

when the sirens went warning that German fighter-planes were coming. A plane was on us before we knew what was happening and they began to machine-gun the ferry. We threw ourselves down on the deck and listened to the shattering of glass and the splintering of wood as the bullets ripped into the boat. Although no one was injured, it was a very frightening experience.

Girl, aged eighteen, Wallasey

1940 DAYLIGHT RAID

It started with the sound of aeroplanes. It was a warm, muggy overcast day and raining. We looked out of the classroom window, and couldn't see a thing. We didn't recognize the *zhoooorzh, zhoooorzh, zhoooorzh* of unsynchronized German engines in those days.

Then the sound of a boy running a stick along a set of iron railings, far away. More boys running iron railings. Then the sound of the aeroplanes went really wild, like they were going to crash above the clouds.

Then the sirens went. We had to run to the surface brick shelter down the street. A sloping wet slippery street, and all the time the sound of invisible planes going mad just above us.

Then a Spitfire came diving down through the clouds, vertically, just above us. We thought it was going to crash on us, but it pulled out just above the rooftops, and flew round and round in circles, as if it was frightened a German had followed it. Then it puts its nose up, and disappeared back into the clouds as vertically as it had come down.

Nobody was watching where they were going; someone stumbled and we all fell over him, and we all arrived in a heap at the door of the shelter, and crawled inside, for the noise of the invisible planes was terrific by now and boys rattling sticks all over the sky.

We kept on trying to nip out to have a quick look; the teacher had to clout one or two for it.

We were sent home when the 'all clear' sounded. The streets were covered with little heavy silver mushrooms – bullets that had flattened themselves as they hit the ground. You could still find them months afterwards, hidden under privet hedges.

The news said that seventeen German raiders had been shot down – but they said the battle had taken place over the Farne Islands, about forty miles north of us.

Boy, aged ten, Tyneside

1939–40 CASUALTIES OF WAR

In 1939 my school was evacuated to Scarborough, but I didn't go, as my parents wished me to stay at home and assist them with our family's holiday camp, as far as a schoolboy could.

One afternoon I was at home, the siren having sounded, and I saw a German bomber circle the lighthouse half a mile away and drop a bomb on Larder's caravan camp. A Mrs Read suffered a fractured arm and leg when the caravan she and her husband shared was flattened by the explosion. Mrs Read moved subsequently to the Kenwood Camp right behind my parents' home, as this was a chalet-camp used for billeting soldiers and bombed-out people, as was our camp. Mrs Read suffered a great shortening of her leg, and had to wear a high-soled boot on recovery.

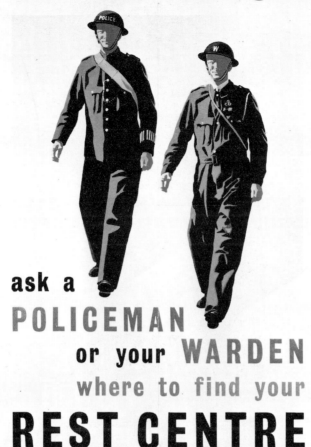

IF YOU ARE BOMBED OUT
and have no friends to go to

ask a
POLICEMAN
or your WARDEN
where to find your
REST CENTRE

One evening at six o'clock I had gone to the Little Kinema with my mother, to see a comedy film. We were inside only a few minutes when the siren went. Shortly afterwards I heard a rushing sound, commenting to my mother that the steam train must have arrived, the cinema being opposite the station. For some reason I was uneasy, and had a strange feeling as I said it, that it was untrue. The next minute we were choking from the dust of two 350 lb. bombs. The blast broke the exit-doors and many people were prevented from leaving by Mr Bob Neil, the local sugar-boiler and rock-maker, who suggested we'd be safer inside than in the streets. This was good judgement as only minutes later the streets were raked with machine-gun fire from the planes, a popular local bus inspector being killed in a hail of fire. Fortunately the main street was deserted due to being tea-time, saving many lives.

Vapour trails: the calligraphy of fighter combat. Spitfires could turn in a tighter circle than Messerschmitts . . .

Later, a lad found an item on the beach and took it to his mother's caravan in Moser's caravan camp. It exploded, sending shrapnel through weather-boards an inch thick. It was a timber caravan, and his mother lost her foot and part of her lower leg as a result of the explosion. The unfortunate lady could be seen being pushed round the town in a wheelchair for many years afterwards. The lad had put it on the table when he came in, not realizing the danger.

Many a night my family would be unable to sleep as we watched the glow of Hull burning and heard the anti-aircraft guns banging away, about fifteen miles as the crow flies. We had an oak dining-table with a top one inch thick with cabriole legs, and we sat under this when we became worried, as the bombers had to pass over our brick bungalow, going to Hull and coming back. Regularly, fresh people would arrive to dwell in our requisitioned timber holiday chalets, having been bombed-out of Hull, many still living there till 1960, when they were found council accommodation.

I played the cornet in the local Gospel Mission Band, being the youngest player at nine. Shortly afterwards, Mr Back the ex-Salvation Army officer who led the Mission was sent to gaol for allegedly spreading rumours, and the Gospel Mission was closed. I believe he was innocent, but the authorities were very jumpy early in the war.

Another gentleman, Mr Benjamin Smith, was also sent to the local cells for one night, as he had been seen on the promenade, using a pair of binoculars, looking out to sea. He was our local radio repair man, usually short of cash, very kind and helpful, possessing a bicycle that was rusty, decrepit and unique. It only had one handlebar, as he found the other handlebar got in the way. So he took a hacksaw and lopped it off, being able to carry a radio under his arm much more easily while on his cycle. There was only one brake left and he used one foot sliding on the road to supplement the existing brake. This caused much hilarity among us schoolboys.

Our local cinema was run by Mr Vincent Lockey, and owing to the petrol shortage he used an electric battery-driven van. It did about ten miles an hour on the level road and made a whining noise that was rather weird in the blackout. I think it was an ex-laundry van.

I went into Hull one day and forgot my gasmask. Unfortunately I was caught in a test with gas, and although I went into a shop to shelter I had to be treated by Civil Defence for severe eye irritation, I never forgot my gasmask again; it taught me a lesson. It was tear-gas.

There was a young mother by the name of Anne Marie who lived in our camp. I did not know her surname or her husband, as he was possibly away in the services. Having been bombed-out in Hull she was allocated to our number 10, and she had a child with her, about five years of age and went to the local infants' school.

About this time the South Promenade, which had received scant maintenance during the war, collapsed one night when the sea was rough, leaving a gap about ninety feet wide, which about doubled in the next fortnight. Two nice bungalows, known as 'La Plaza' and 'Kingdom's Café', ended up on the beach as the sea ate into the land to a depth of fifty feet.

One day Anne Marie's child was seen playing near the gap in the sea-wall. The next thing the mother knew was the child had disappeared. What happened may never be known – in spite of police inquiries, searches by local people, etc., the child was never seen again. It is almost certain the child was drowned or maybe buried by a fresh fall of earth from under the promenade paving-stone decking but no trace was ever found.

It was the custom to gather money for a wreath in the camp if anyone was bereaved, but what can you do if there is no funeral? Everyone in the camp was very upset, as was the whole town at the time. May the little one rest in peace, may perpetual light shine on the little one!

Boy, aged nine, Withernsea, Humberside

CHAPTER 8 THE LONDON BLITZ

SEPT 1940 THE BEGINNING OF THE BLITZ

A squadron of Heinkel 111K bombers were approaching with Me 109 escorts. Six Spitfires thundered over to intercept. In the ensuing battle the bombers were dispersed, the remains of six German and two English planes were scattered over our town. A stick of three 250 lb. bombs had fallen close by and we walked around to see the damage. Only one had fallen near a house. The owner showed us the ruined furniture, the broken window and door frames, and the large hole in his garden.

It was our first experience of air attack and I think it gave us a false sense of security. We felt if this was the worst German bombs can do we needn't worry.

On that day we mourned the two pilots who had died in the battle over our heads (they were Polish).

The following Saturday, 7 Sept., the siren sounded again.

It was obviously no repeat of the previous week. The sky was full of approaching bombers. As we watched we could see their bomb-racks opening and bombs beginning to fall. We took to the Anderson shelter in our garden, taking turns to peer out of the door to see what was happening. It was obvious from the noise that bombs were not being aimed at specific targets, but were being dropped in an indiscriminate carpet over the civilians of London.

My brother was at work in the Siemens factory at Charlton and my mother was very concerned for his safety. She kept saying 'If we are to be killed, at least we should all be killed together.'

The raid ended about 18.30 hours. We emerged from the

We shared a shelter with a fireman's wife. Every time she heard the fire-engine bells, she said: 'The Jerries aim their bombs at the fires.'

shelter to take stock. Our house wasn't damaged, but an unexploded shell had gone through the house opposite and the road had to be closed until the bomb-disposal men could shift it. Over the river great fires had been started and as darkness fell a red glow lit the area.

About 19.30 hours the sirens went again and we were to hear the start of a winter of endless bombardment. The attacking bombers concentrated on the areas where fires still raged, and further fires were started. We felt sorry for the East Enders who were really 'copping a packet'.

Schools were reopened for children still remaining in London; much of our time was spent in the air-raid shelter, which paradoxically was a cloakroom, with bricked-up windows, three storeys up in the building!

The nightly raids meant that even though we had beds in the shelter we didn't get much sleep. The early bombers would drop incendiaries. If these were not put out the following bombers would drop high explosives. It became necessary to organize firewatchers to quickly extinguish any that fell. My brother organized street-watches. I typed the rotas, which were displayed on hand-made notice-boards around the district.

Once we were showered with individual bombs – there were three on our house alone – one under the car. We quickly put out all visible light. It was only then that one was discovered lodged in the roof of the house next door, owned by an old couple. It had no access to the roof area. The old people were in the shelter and had not been disturbed. We gained entry and located the bomb. We could see the glow through the ceiling in their bedroom. A metal bucket was placed underneath and the ceiling around the fire cut through with a water-jet from the stirrup-pump until the bomb eventually fell through.

When it was all over my brother found that he was wearing his slippers on the wrong feet!

Not all incidents were without humour – a string of incendiaries fell in the cemetery and our firewatchers climbed over the walls to put them out. They were using flower-pots and whatever was to hand. However, on achieving this they successfully eliminated all light and were unable to find their way out again!

No doubt the relatives of those occupying the graves would have blamed vandals for the emptying of the flower-pots, had it not been for the little piles of grey ash and metal fins left from the bombs.

We knew that parachute flares overhead could mean we had

been selected for punishment that night; therefore lights in the sky were viewed with alarm. One night whilst bedded down in our shelter, a light appeared to hang in the sky. We watched it for a considerable time before we realized it was a glow-worm crawling over the curtain which we had fitted to the opening – quite a relief . . .

Every day brought its own tale of war. We became like a village and tended to disregard the troubles of others three or four streets away.

A bomb fell further up the road, taking out two houses and killing the lodger in one. He had just run indoors from the shelter to make a cup of tea.

Remarkably, the houses on either side were undamaged, although further away roofs were broken by descending debris. The front doorstep of one of the houses came through the roof of the house next door, finishing up on the landing, leaving a gaping hole to the sky. Naturally, next day it rained. Our neighbour, after removing the huge lump of concrete, put a tin bath at the top of the stairs to collect the rain. Their teenage son came out of the bathroom, fell over the half-filled bath and accompanied it downstairs, to the consternation of his mother!

A nose-cap of an anti-aircraft shell penetrated our roof and lodged through the ceiling of the bathroom. When removed this left a small round hole through which dust dribbled when an explosion occurred near by.

The fixed gun installations had been augmented by mobile units who would roar up the road, clamp down, and fire a few salvoes before rushing off elsewhere. I don't think they ever shot any enemy planes down, but it helped morale considerably.

Nightly the raids continued unabated. During the day through intermittent raids I attended school, spending most of the time in the third-floor cloakroom shelter. Once we were violently shaken by a very near miss. As we left school we saw the rescue teams, ambulances etc., at the factory next door. The bomb had fallen down the ventilation shaft into the shelter where the factory girls had been assembled. The dead and injured were being removed; the carnage was horrible. It was a sobering thought that only 10 feet separated us from suffering that fate. I decided that after I had taken the pending exams I would have to learn First Aid.

I did well in the exams and was one of two to obtain a Grammar School pass. I was sent to Colfes Grammar School at

Lewisham, which throughout the war was called SELESSFB (South East London Emergency Secondary School for Boys).

Boy, aged twelve, London

1940 UNNAMED HORRORS

The things that are going on now in these public air-raid shelters are very dreadful. For a young girl to go into a public shelter now without her father and mother is simply asking for trouble.

London magistrate reported in Evening Standard, *4 November 1940*

1940 UNDERGROUND PEOPLE

On 7 September, the bombers came early. That day stands out as a great flaming wound in my memory. Imagine a ground-floor flat, crowded with hysterical women, crying babies, great crashes in the sky and the whole earth shaking. Someone rushed in.

'The docks are alight. All the docks are alight.' I could smell the burning.

'Trust the poor to get it in the neck, why don't they sort out the rich?'

The men started to play cards and the women tried a little sing-song – 'I saw the old homestead and faces I loved' or 'Yiddle mit his fiddle'. But every so often, twenty women's fists shook at the ceiling, cursing the explosions, Germany, Hitler.

'May he die from a lingering tumour,' my mother wailed.

'That's too good for him,' Aunt Sarah said. Yes, cursing got my mother and aunts through those early days. I sat under the table where the men were playing cards, screwing up my eyes and covering my ears, counting the explosions.

'We're all gonna be killed, we're finished.' One of my aunts became hysterical.

'Churchill will get us through, he's a friend of the Yiddisher people.' With these words she was soothed.

This time all my uncles nodded agreement, even the Marxist playing Solo.

The all-clear sounded a beautiful symphony in my ears.

After the terror of that night, people started to flock towards the tube. They wanted to get underground. Thousands upon thousands the next evening pushed their way into Liverpool Street Station, demanding to be let down to shelter. At first the

Jewish men studying the Scriptures during an air raid. This is not a real shelter – only an old and crumbling cellar under a large house. When the building collapsed on them, they were lethal.

So many, so close, so private, so relaxed: a London underground station.

authorities wouldn't agree, and called out the soldiers to bar the way. I stood there in the thick of the crowd, thinking there would be a panic and we would all be crushed to death.

It was the worst experience I had up till then and I wanted to rush out of that crowd, but I was jammed tight. I would have preferred to take my chances in the street with the bombs. Anything was preferable to that crush. I shouted my head off, went limp and was carried along by the surging masses, trying to hold on to my separate identity. The people would not give up and would not disperse, would not take no for an answer. A great yell went up and the gates were opened and my mother threw her hands together and clutched them towards the sky. 'Thank God, he heard me.' As if she had a special line to Him and He had intervened with the Government on behalf of the Kops family.

'It's a great victory for the working class,' a man said.

So I dashed with the crowd into the underground and saw the solidarity of the surface disappear as an endless stream of people crushed in after us. We were underground people with the smell of disinfectant in our nostrils and blankets under our arms, standing jammed, shoving and pushing each other. No laughter, no humour. What sort of victory had we achieved? Every family for itself now, and my mother trying to encompass all her family with her bulk, a family that had emigrated into the bowels of the earth. Dignity and joy left the world. Shuffling down, I felt as if I were fulfilling some awful prophecy. Something that everybody knew, but didn't want to talk about.

The soldiers downstairs forced us on to trains, to go further up the line. Liverpool Street, being the closest, was the most popular. So we were forced to move on and we tried the next station along the Central Line, then the next and the next.

I heard sirens. And sirens and sirens. Early in the morning, in the afternoon and in the evening. And we went underground to get away from the sirens and the bombs. Yet they followed me and I heard sirens until the world became a siren. One endless cry of torture. It penetrated right into the core of my being, night and day was one long night, one long nightmare, one long siren, one long wail of despair.

I would scoot out of the train ahead of the family and under the legs of people, unravelling the three or four scarves tied round me. And I bagged any space I could along the platform. The family followed, and we pitched our 'tent' and unwound and relaxed. Out came the sandwiches and the forced good humour. Here we were, involved in a new exodus – the Jews of the East End, gone into exile in the underground. Our spirits would

No room left on the platform: safety at the price of torment. Piccadilly Station, 1940.

rise for a while, we were alive for another night, we would see another dawn.

Now I see that the miracle of Moses wasn't getting the message from God but in getting all the Jews to go in the same direction, one big happy family. For despite the friendliness and sharing of sandwiches, families were going in all directions, each trying to feather its own three feet of concrete. And something had been lost without trace. This is what Hitler had brought to London. The Jewish people of London with their terrific communal feeling were being torn apart, irrevocably for all time. But then, so was the whole world.

'This is what they brought to the world,' my mother said. And an old man with a sharp beard sitting down next to me, shook his head knowingly. 'When they start on the Jews a terrible retribution comes to the world. Look at Haman! Look at Pharoah!'

But I wasn't only miserable; for seizing advantage of my

mother's pre-occupations, I managed to get some money out of her. And I got bars and bars of chocolate out of the chocolate machines, and weighed myself incessantly. Here was a new life, a whole network, a whole city under the world. We rode up and down the escalators. The children of London were adapting themselves to the times, inventing new games, playing hopscotch while their mothers shyly suckled babies on the concrete. And I used to ride backwards and forwards in the trains, to see the other stations of underground people.

One night, though, we were very lucky. We were pitched down at Liverpool Street and Phyllis and I decided to venture as far as Marble Arch. As the train moved out of Bank station and entered the tunnel, it stopped and all the lights went out. There was a great thud and we held our ears. When we returned we realized a bomb had fallen down the lift shaft of that station and, apart from those killed by the blast, there were also those who had been thrown on the line and electrocuted, just as our train pulled out.

From Bernard Kops, The World is a Wedding (*McGibbon and Kee, 1963*)

1940 GETTING USED TO AIR RAIDS

Games at school were liable to be enlivened by dog-fights between aircraft overhead and it was sometimes necessary to run for cover as a stream of bullets ploughed across the pitch. However we were soon back collecting cartridge cases.

On one occasion, being in the sitting-room with the family, I looked up from my book to see nothing but a bouncing ball of wool, unravelling behind my mother who had disappeared for the shelter with the rest of them. I sauntered through to learn that they had heard the whistle of a bomb which I, absorbed in my book, had not. We did not hear the explosion, but next day discovered that it had gone clean through into the basement of the mayor's house two roads away and killed the entire family.

Boy, aged eleven, Home Counties

1940 THE NIGHT THE BOMB FELL

Late autumn; we had yellow chrysanthemums on our sitting-room windowsill. That night the grown-ups in our shelter kept saying the raid was specially heavy. 'One night they *will* get the railway line,' said Mother. It was common knowledge that the railway line a quarter of a mile away carried ammunition trains from the factory at Park Royal.

There was a tremendous bang, and the shelter lights went out. I expected the shelter to collapse, but nothing hit me. We heard bricks falling, people shouting.

'My God, we're hit,' screamed Mother, and immediately got out of the shelter. Then she leant back in, outlined by searchlights.

'Come out,' she said. 'I don't believe it.'

We climbed up the ladder. All the hens were cackling wildly and flapping. Fires in the distance, but everything looked the same as usual. We ran up the back-garden path and through the house. Just then my uncle came in the front door.

'Keep those children in,' he shouted. But we all ran past him.

There was a huge hole opposite – two houses down, looking like teeth that needed filling in the semi-dark. Bricks were still falling and a ring of wardens shouting 'Keep back, keep back!' to the people who were pouring in, from up and down the street.

Then Mr Leggatt was helped out of the ruins of his house, bleeding round the head. Then his son, with only a scratch on his hand.

After a long time, bombs falling all round, whistles blowing, planes roaring, searchlights picking out planes and barrage balloons overhead, the ambulance came. A stretcher was carried out, the body covered over completely. Then another, but the face showing, covered with blood.

'It's Margaret,' everyone whispered. 'Then Mrs Leggatt is dead.'

'Here – what about the Jones, next door?'

'They're all away.'

'It's a miracle.'

A warden yelled at my mother 'Get those kids indoors – there's a bloody raid going on!'

Margaret and Mr Leggatt had been folding a tablecloth by the larder door. Dozens of jars and bottles had been blown into fragments, and Margaret was still having operations five years after the war to remove the glass. She was eighteen.

All our downstairs windows were broken, but for some reason, the upstairs ones weren't. The broken glass had got into the yellow chrysanthemums. My mother immediately picked it all out, and they lived for three more weeks. The house was thick with fallen soot. Precious, my doll, had a white Victorian frilled nightie that had to be destroyed, it was so filthy. I *hated* Hitler.

After the bomb site had been tidied up, our gang used to play there and have secret fires. Until one day a woman saw us and said 'That's where Mrs Leggatt died. You kids ought to be

The East End High Anglican clergy, fathers of their huge slum parishes in peace, proved pillars of strength in war.

Wood for rabbit hutches; wood for fires; waste not, want not.

ashamed.' We never went there again to play, but set up a little stone and put flowers on it in summer, and leaves in winter, and holly at Christmas.

Fatty Waller said we ought to send Margaret Christmas cards, so we all told our mums we were being kept in at school, and went up to Willesden Hospital with them. They took the cards, but they wouldn't let us see her.

On Christmas Eve we all went to the bomb site and sang 'Away in a Manger', then

> Whistle while you work
> Hitler is a twerp
> Goering's barmy
> So's his army
> Whistle while you work.

Then we didn't know what to do, so we all went home, and got into trouble for being so dirty.

Girl, aged six, London

Wherever the disasters were worst, they were there, listening. When Buckingham Palace was bombed, the Queen said she was glad. 'Now we can look the East End in the face.' This photograph was taken in South London, October 1940.

1940   IN THE SHELTER

We had an Anderson shelter at the bottom of the garden. The three of us shared it with Maude and Laura Rowlands (two maiden ladies who lived next door) and their fat old brown-and-white mongrel, Patch. It was very damp. My mother caught lumbago from the damp and eczema from spring-cleaning with washing-soda, as there was no soap to be had. Every morning she had to drag herself backwards up the shelter steps, in time to make our breakfast before we went to school. If you were late, and there hadn't been a raid the night before, you got caned. Fortunately we lived by the railway. There were raids every night.

Girl, aged six, London

1940 LANDMINE

We were all in our shelters, and in spite of an air raid some miles away, most of us were asleep. Suddenly there was a lot of whistling, men shouting 'Everyone to the front of their houses'. Then a loud-hailer. 'This is the police – everyone to the front of their houses, PLEASE.'

My mother said 'They must be mad, with an air raid going on.'

'Perhaps the Germans have invaded?'

When we got to the front, wardens and police were telling everyone they had ten minutes to get out of their houses and go to friends at least half a mile away. If they didn't know anyone, they were to go to Harvist Road School – *my* school. There was an unexploded landmine in Doyle Gardens and as soon as all the neighbouring roads had been evacuated, they would be closed, so the Army could move in. 'Be as quick as you can – DO NOT WAIT TO DRESS. Turn off your gas, electricity and water. If you can find your pets take them. Do not waste time looking for them. Take your ration-books, if you can find them quickly. Take what blankets you can carry.'

'Granny's,' said Mother. The warden marched alongside us; we were all still in our nightclothes. The raid was now overhead. Ack-ack guns fired from Roundwood Park. We heard a plane crashing. Searchlights all over the sky.

'I'm frightened, Mr Leggatt,' I said to the warden.

'Here's my tin hat,' he said, putting it on me.

'I want one,' said my brother. He was only four, and my mother kept carrying him, then putting him down. Mr Leggatt left us, to hurry other people on. One woman was carrying a budgie . . .

It didn't feel like half a mile – more like ten. Grandmother lived near Harvist Road. She was very frightened, being knocked up at two in the morning, as my uncle was a warden and she thought he'd been killed.

The pram was a refuge, a rallying point, the family transport; wearing an adult tin hat for a few minutes an enormous privilege.

My mother gave her the big blanket, and she settled mother on the couch in the living-room, and my brother on cushions on the floor by her side. Then she wrapped me up in the big blanket, found a pillow and put me to bed in the bath. I went to sleep at once, the helmet beside me.

I dreamt I was drowning, slowly. Then I awoke to find the cold tap dripping in my face. 'I can't go to school in my nightie!' I told my mother.

'Don't be silly,' said mother. 'They're using the school as an Emergency Shelter.' She borrowed clothes for herself from Granny and went out. Granny made me and my brother a huge breakfast.

My uncle came home. 'They've not moved the damned thing,' he said. Mother returned, carrying clothes for my brother and me – some borrowed from friends, some bought without coupons, with a promise to take coupons as soon as she could.

'I had to pay Mr Spillman double for this dress,' she said.

'I don't like it,' I whined.

Crack! 'Don't be so ungrateful,' she said. I knew better than to argue – it would only mean another smack.

That afternoon we wandered down to the school to see our friends. Many were still in their nightclothes. Mrs Murphy, who had *six* children, had them all in day-clothes, and herself. People said afterwards they never wore nightclothes, just in case . . .

Two days later, three army cars came to Harvist Road School to say the Army had taken the landmine away. We could go home. Only then we found the ack-ack gun in Roundwood Park had received a direct hit. So that was what the Germans had been aiming for.

'Would we all have been killed,' asked my brother, 'if it had gone bang?'

'Depends,' said my mother, and got on with peeling the potatoes.

Girl, aged six, London

AUTUMN
AUTUMN 1940 BEING BOMBED

A nasty nervous feeling in the kitchen. Every thud, Mrs R would say 'Is that a bomb?', and Mr R would say 'No, it's a gun, dear.' As time went on, they'd said it so often Mr R would answer 'No s'a gun', then just 'S'a gun', then finally a noise that sounded like 'S'gun'. She could see he was getting irritated and tried not to do it; muttering the question under her breath instead; which of course made it more irritating still. I felt all swollen up with irritation, bloated, but actually it was fear.

E says to me 'Let's get some air.' Out we go . . . a beautiful summer night, so warm it was incredible and made more beautiful than ever by the red glow from the east, where the docks were burning. I tried to fix the scene in my mind, because one day this will be history.

I wasn't frightened any more, amazing. Being out in the open, you feel more in control when you can see what's happening. The searchlights were beautiful, it's like watching the end of the world as they swoop from one end of the sky to the other. We didn't see any planes, though we could hear them bumbling about somewhere.

We sat on the grass. Very long and unkempt – Mr R is normally a besotted gardener, but he has let the garden go to rack and ruin this summer . . . the uncertainty.

Two bombs fell in the distance. I felt no fear. E said he could smell burning from the docks.

Another bomb, nearer. Then, suddenly, the weirdest scratching sound just above the roofs – as if someone was scratching the sky with a broken fingernail. Then the most God-awful crash – it seemed only a couple of gardens away, I felt the earth juddering under me as I sat.

'Hey, it's not too healthy out here!' E dragged me up from the grass. I didn't seem to be doing *anything* – just cowering. I don't know what I meant to do, or what I was feeling ... a funny blank.

I remember racing towards the house, E pulling me and yelling. The oddest feeling in the air all around, as if the whole air was falling apart, quite silently. And then suddenly I was on my face, just inside the kitchen door. There seemed to be waves buffeting me, one after another, like bathing in a rough sea. I remember clutching at the floor, the carpet, to prevent myself being swept away. This smell of carpet in my nose and trying not to be swept away, and I could hear Mrs R screaming. E was nowhere, the lights were gone, it was all dust, I didn't even wonder if he was all right ... didn't give him a thought. Seemed to be nothing in the universe but this dusty carpet I was breathing and having to hang on like grim death. I clutched the floor as if it was a cliff-face; why I had this feeling of saving myself from falling, I don't know. Mrs R seemed to have been crying for

This terrace had fallen like a pack of cards.

ages, and calling out something or other, but I couldn't think of answering her. I discovered later my mouth was full of plaster and dust, but I had no feeling of that at the time. I just didn't *think* of answering or doing anything about anything. Almost a tranquil feeling. I could hear Mr R yelling: 'Down, everybody, get *down*. Do what I tell you, get your heads down!' Over and over – no sense in it, because we'd had the bomb now and everybody was down, heads and all.

E had a torch, he flashed it round a bit. Plaster and glass everywhere, mountains. The whole ceiling had come down, it looked like a builder's yard. You couldn't see the furniture, only the clock and a cushion sticking out. Mr R was still shouting, giving orders, very contradictory. 'Don't move, stay where you are! Someone tell the H's next door. Don't move till I tell you!' and so on, and so on.

We got to the front door, quite a job as the ceilings were down right along the passage, and pitch dark. I could hear Mrs R stumbling along behind, Mr R scolding her, 'Watch out – can't you look where you're going?', every time she stumbled. Actually, he was stumbling just as much, and he's normally a very amiable, detached, good-natured sort of man who rarely raises his voice.

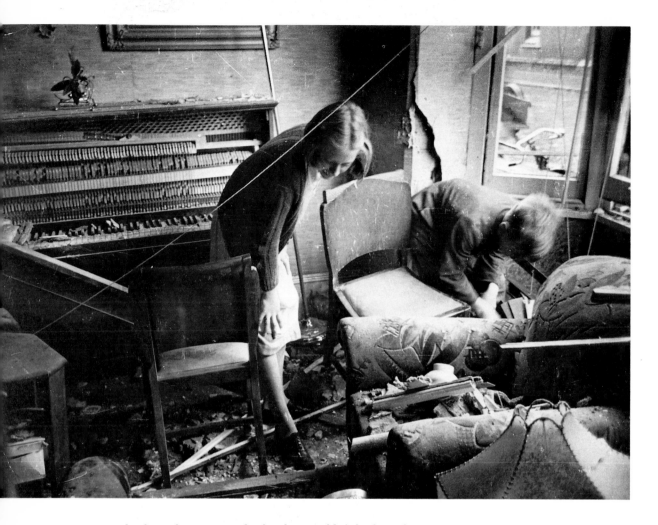

... and belongings ...

The front door was wedged tight, wouldn't budge. There were men outside and someone saying in a high-pitched voice 'Naomi, ask Naomi, Naomi will know. Has anyone seen Naomi?'

We went back through the front room, it wasn't so bad there, the ceiling had held and we crawled out through a broken window. It looked so bright outside I couldn't believe it, a sort of white haze, a halo over everything, though there was no moon. Two of the women cried when they saw us; how terrible we must have looked, smothered in white plaster all over, and streaks of blood from the glass. 'Are you hurt ... are you all right?' people kept asking. It was only then that it occurred to me I *might* have been hurt – I had been in *actual danger*. Up to that minute I had taken everything for granted, in a queer brainless way, as if it were all perfectly ordinary.

We spent the night at the F's, Mrs F insisting on piling about seven blankets on top of me, and a hot-water bottle as well.

... and pets.

'For the shock,' she said. When I pointed out that I was feeling perfectly all right, she referred darkly to '*delayed*' shock, implying this dread phenomenon would hit me before the night was out.

It didn't. I lay there feeling indescribably happy and triumphant.

'I've been *bombed*,' I kept saying to myself, over and over – trying the phrase on like a new dress, to see how it fitted. 'I've been bombed – me.'

It seems a terrible thing to say, when so many must have been killed, but never in my life have I experienced such *pure and flawless happiness*.

Young girl, London. Taken from Tom Harrison (Mass Observation),
Living through the Blitz, *Collins, 1976.*

1943   ARP MESSENGER

I joined the St John's Cadets, but found I was mostly being chosen as a casualty; finding myself bound head to foot whilst others broke for tea. So I decided I would be more useful in the Civil Defence as a messenger. The District Warden, a Mr W.H. Munday, suggested that though I was well under age, they could use me at my local wardens' post. I joined Post KK6 in early 1942 and accompanied the Post Warden on his patrols.

My job was to ensure communication between the incident and the wardens' post, should a bomb fall in our area.

Early in 1943 there was one of the strike raids and our home area was saturated with incendiary bombs by the first plane in. We worked tirelessly to extinguish the light from the fires before the next planes came over. We achieved this, although a couple of wardens were hurt by the anti-personnel devices, the worst being the German flower-pot bomb, which consisted of an assortment of prisms and flower-pot shaped incendiaries, surrounding a small but lethal explosive device, timed to explode and kill the firefighters.

I was patrolling with the Post Warden, when we came upon a man running hysterically along the road. We eventually ascertained that as he was sitting in his front room a vivid green flash occurred in his hall, together with a loud crashing. He had been so startled that he jumped clean through the glass of his front window.

Surely enough the front window was broken. On entering the hall we found the wallpaper and woodwork had been burnt. A hole through the roof marked the passage of the bomb, and a further hole running under the house showed its direction of travel. We knew that we had here a phosphorus bomb; a canister filled with a chemical which burns when exposed to air, but can be extinguished in water, only to burn again once it is dry. The bomb was buried under the house in soft earth and was leaking slightly. We notified bomb-disposal, but they were completely occupied and couldn't come for at least a week.

To save this house from burning, and perhaps the whole district from further attack, we had to ensure this bomb did not ignite. At fourteen I was by far the smallest member of Civil Defence, and therefore most able to crawl through the tunnel made by the bomb.

I was given a bucket of water, which I pushed ahead of me, until I came to the tail of the bomb. I then tipped the water over the bomb and retreated. Twice a day, until it could be rendered safe.

We also had unexploded HE. Two of these were in the centre of Flaxton Road. It was customary to see groups of young mothers with their babies in prams, gathering round the two holes to watch the disposal men as they worked. They had lost all sense of fear – unfortunately.

There was a third, which wasn't found until the Saturday, long after the other two had been made harmless. This was in the front garden of a house in our road – the occupants were away – on the Saturday my mother had carried out a long conversation, not two feet from the weapon. That evening it was discovered to be in a dangerous condition.

In the clearing up, we discovered a nearly complete canister of incendiaries in a playing field close to the wardens' post. I held my arms out as the wardens loaded up the unexploded incendiaries. With about twenty-five of these little monsters I started to walk back to the post, being careful to see that the pins which activated them didn't fall out in the process.

I kept one of them as a souvenir. One day I took it to school in the saddlebag of my bike and showed it to my friends there. It passed from hand to hand and during assembly one of the 'wags' saw fit to test it by dropping it to the floor. The bomb detonated and the chaos that resulted ... the hall filled with smoke and the boys evacuated it in record time to reassemble in the courtyard.

The porter, in his zeal, up-ended a chemical fire extinguisher and played it on the fire. This caused the bomb to explode and shower burning particles over the end of the hall. It was eventually put out, but left a crater in the parquet flooring and damaged the Honours List.

We reassembled, and prayers continued as if there had been no interruption – no mention was made of the incident. After assembly I grabbed the fellow who had dropped the bomb and we reported to the Head – he to say he'd dropped it and me to say I'd brought it. We were sent to his study, where my accomplice chickened out and said it was an accident; he was excused. I, naturally, felt I was really in for it. Dr Reece suspended me and sent me home. When I told my father he took it very well and immediately phoned Dr Reece. His eloquence enabled me to return to school, where I was viewed with caution by the staff and admiration by the boys.

Being a district group, we also assisted in training exercises, usually acting as 'casualties' in staged incidents. One of my messengers was dropped from a building and broke an arm while being 'rescued' by the trainee team. For my pains I was put under a derelict house which was collapsed above me. There was a label attached to my coat which stated 'coal-gas poisoning, not breathing'. I lay there for what seemed an age, covered in dust under the stairs, completely entombed, whilst the 'rescuers' dug for me. Not a very nice experience. When light started to filter through I noticed a newspaper dated 1927 lying beside me. I could not help but moralize, that being the year of my birth.

I was eventually dragged from the ruins and laid on the brick-strewn path whilst being given artificial respiration. My ribs were bruised both front and back. I did not volunteer again!

Another task we had was to umpire the war-games between the Army and the Home Guard, the former being attackers and the latter defenders of London. The former always won, as there was a hot cup of tea for prisoners!

Once, we set up our observation post in a bush alongside the cemetery, at a junction of two footpaths, and settled for a long night. My colleague was a local barber, a Jew with a very fierce manner.

He fell asleep, and started to snore. I kept watch. About 2.30 a.m. I heard the cautious approach of a number of men. As they drew near I woke Jack in case his snores betrayed our position. He had been dreaming about German paratroops. He came to with a roar and leapt from the bush.

The six-man patrol, confronted with a black figure (Civil Defence uniform was dark blue) leaping from out of the cemetery in the middle of the night, dropped their rifles and fled. I understand they gave themselves up to the first opposing patrol. Jack and I were in hysterics when we realized the implication – that cemetery was a very frightening place.

Boy, aged sixteen, London

CHAPTER 9 THE PROVINCIAL BLITZ

1941 SINGING HYMNS

I don't remember feeling really frightened, though the first sound of the sirens produced a slightly odd sensation in the stomach. Only one thing really frightened me, the devilish shriek of a bomb equipped with screaming-fins. My parents said reassuringly that it was a passing anti-aircraft shell. Somehow, if it was 'one of ours' its closeness didn't seem to matter so much.

On the night of the screaming bombs we were in our coalhouse shelter at the height of the raid when the grown-ups began singing hymns. 'Good fun,' I thought, and joined in lustily. When the novelty wore off, I announced that I wanted to sing all by myself. Of course, they said. But every time I got halfway through a verse, they started to sing too. I grew more and more exasperated. They weren't usually so perverse. Yet each time I protested and begged and they solemnly promised, they would break the promise a moment later. I never suspected they were drowning out the next flight of screaming bombs, so I wouldn't be terrified. But they needn't have bothered; after their comforting little lie I wasn't worried anyway.

Another time we were all sitting at the meal-table by the kitchen window when a solitary aircraft came over. It was broad daylight and no sirens had sounded. Suddenly my father said 'That's a Jerry. I can tell by the engine. Better get under the table.' I duly took my cup of tea and squatted between the table legs with my back to the wall. Just as I had settled comfortably the plane dropped a landmine. There was a tremendous explosion and every ack-ack gun in the neighbourhood opened up. My family were out of their chairs and under the table in a single movement. In the midst of all the hubbub my voice rose in a protesting wail. 'Mind my cup of tea!' The whole family collapsed under the table, helpless with laughter.

Boy, aged ten, Manchester

1941   A NASTY ONE

My father came off duty looking pale and sick, and said the Germans had scored a direct hit on Wilkinson's Lemonade Factory, and hundreds had been killed, and some were still trapped down there in the cellars. He said there should never have been a shelter down there. There'd been heavy bottling machinery on the ground floor, just standing on wooden boards, and when the bomb hit, it all just collapsed on the people below.

Terrible rumours started going round. People so crushed they couldn't be recognized; people sitting down there without a mark on them, just dead. Mothers with babies still in their arms. A man still holding his accordion . . .

Everybody was just stunned; couldn't cope. Why had God let it happen?

Then the stories changed. Wicked things had gone on in that shelter. People had taken drink down there; held parties. Music and dancing every night. Immorality, and they didn't care who saw it . . . People went there even when there wasn't a raid going on. Gambling . . .

People said it was a Judgement. God is not mocked! It was like Sodom and Gomorrah.

Everybody felt much better after that.

Boy, aged twelve, Tyneside

1941–4   WINDFALLS

My earliest recollection was a bright red glow in the sky from my bedroom window. 'Are you frightened?' whispered my brother.

No, I just couldn't understand the sun rising so late at night. Next morning we discovered it was an RAF plane that had crashed on to the cricket pitch at the back of the 'Bull's Head'. Just a mass of twisted metal burnt beyond recognition with one wheel sticking up like a toffee-apple. Did he crash on to the cricket pitch to avoid the houses? It was a dark night, how could he have seen it?

The next plane I saw crash was also RAF. Brought down by a barrage balloon operated by WAAFs on the common at the

126

top of our road. I watched it fall, twisting round like a sycamore pod, till it finally disappeared behind the houses. The local fire-engine was on the scene within minutes; I followed behind on my bike and arrived in time to watch them carry away the pilot's body covered by a blanket. The plane crashed on allotments surrounded by houses; another miracle.

Underground shelters were built in Primrose Hill Park. I spent many a long night in those shelters, listening to bombs dropping and an old man playing the accordion.

My mother took my younger brother and I to Evesham, to escape the bombing. Dad stayed behind working in the Daimler factory. We stayed with friends living over a cobbler's shop. My mother's friend, who I called Aunty, had a son my age called Donald. Next door lived a witch. Don and I discovered a way into the Witch's House; up into the attic, across the sloping slate roof and into the witch's attic window. Lo and behold, treasures beyond our wildest dreams! Cardboard boxes, dozens. We opened one – candles. In the next, tins of peaches. In the next, pears, pineapples, plums. On a rainy day we spent many a happy hour in the witch's attic, eating tinned fruit by the light of a candle.

One night, Aunty's husband came home drunk and locked Mum and us out of the house. We went to the Police Station and a very large sergeant took us back.

'Open in the name of the law!' said the bobby to the door, and we were let in. Next day, Dad came to visit us. Later I noticed Aunty's husband had a black eye; good old Dad!

Mum and my brother returned to Coventry, leaving me with Aunty. I have unpleasant memories: standing outside the cake-shop window with my nose pressed against the glass; sitting in the park watching a father and son having a picnic, and me eating the pork pie they left behind. My mother found another house in Coventry, I was sent for and the raids started again.

I found an old rusty bike in the shed of the new house and painted it silver; to me it was the best bike in the world. Riding through Brinklow Woods we found an unexploded bomb. Small enough to fit on the crossbar of my bike. We tied it on with string and covered it with my coat, and set off for home. We had to cycle through the city centre with the bomb between my legs. The string snapped, and the nose of the bomb fell on to the lug that holds the bike pump on to the frame, and bent it.

'I can tell people a bomb did that, can't I?'

We tied it on again, and arrived at Derek's house. We dug a hole in the back garden and stood the bomb upright in it, covering it with soil. I told Derek to go and tell his father, who happened to be an ARP warden, that there was a hole in the garden. He came out a few seconds later, followed by his father.

'Look, there it is,' said Derek, pointing a very soily finger at the hole. His father bent down and scooped away a little soil, exposing the fin. He stood up with his mouth wide open; no sound came from him. I looked at Derek; Derek looked at me. Still not a word from his father; his mouth was still wide open.

'Sta ... stand still,' he finally spluttered, and ran into the house. Derek put his hand over his mouth, stifling a laugh. His father reappeared with his ARP helmet on. 'Out of the garden, quick, it's an unexploded bomb.' We ran out and stood across the road. The Bomb Disposal Squad came and took it away. We never told him it was our bomb.

Schooldays were awful, but I could escape by volunteering for potato-picking. I'd turn up for school in old ragged clothes, get my name ticked off, and then grab the back seat of the coach. Lucy sat next to me; I fancied her in my youthful way. Not like they do nowadays (I never thought about it then). The coach took us to Kenilworth. The tractor dug the spuds up, and we filled the sacks. Hard work but better than school. At lunchtime a large bucket of cocoa was brought round; it was foul, no sugar, no milk – but we drank it.

There was an Italian POW camp near by. We took potatoes to the POWs and they fried chips in butter for us. I haven't had chips as good as that since. Happy days! Sugar was rationed; I had treacle in my tea. I still have all my own teeth. I remember a boy at school had a banana. Where he got it I never found out. A lot of kids had never seen one, never mind tasting one. Anyway, after he'd polished it off and thrown the skin away, I picked it up and kept that skin till it turned black and snapped in half.

And of course we had the cinema. The 'Rex' was in the centre of town, one of the largest. *Gone with the Wind* was the latest film showing ...

The enemy obliged; it was destroyed that night by a stick of bombs.

American soldiers appeared in the streets, the place was full of them. They had smart uniforms and big cigars; I thought they were all officers. They all chewed gum; us kids would say 'Any gum, chum?' They always obliged. They played baseball in the park. We called it rounders, a girl's game. I collected cigarette packets they threw away, Camel, Lucky Strike and many others. Then aeroplanes towing gliders with white stripes on the wings flew across Coventry and there wasn't an American in sight. It was D-Day, the sixth of June.

Boy, Coventry

1941 THE NEW SHELTER

The wail of the siren brought my mother upstairs, to shepherd us down. This was great fun! We tipped our old settee on its ends; this was to protect our heads, the three of us! The big old kitchen table was pushed up to it. Hey presto, a home-made air-raid shelter! We cuddled down into makeshift sleeping-bags. The living-room fire was kept on. We were cosy, warm and safe.

Girl, aged nine, Cheshire

1941 A GERMAN MISTAKE

I was rather young when war started – twelve – and it seemed a very exciting time. Although I lived in Ireland, a neutral country then, I experienced one nasty time when the horror of war was brought to my notice.

My brother and I were going to bed when we heard the drone of aircraft overhead. Anti-aircraft guns began to fire and searchlights scanned the sky. We rushed to the window and were watching all of this when suddenly flares began to light up the surrounding areas. Then we heard the whine of bombs falling. Suddenly there was a tremendous explosion and we scampered under the bed. Next morning we heard it had devastated an area half a mile away, killing many people, and smaller bombs had been dropped on the outskirts of the city.

Boy, aged twelve, Dublin

1941 MISSED AGAIN

I lived in Dublin, and the Germans used to drop bombs now and again. An important Jew lived in hiding in Dublin and I did know him. But no Germans knew he was there, we thought. We went down to the club on Fridays. And when this Jew went home, his house had been bombed down. So he went to his friend and stayed there. Well, the next Friday came and we went out as usual, and when he got back to his new house, it was gone again. When he saw this he said,

'Well, they missed me again!'

Boy, aged eight, Dublin

1940　THE WAR IN EDINBURGH

The morning after Dunkirk, there was a bren-gun carrier in our school bike-shed, under a tarpaulin. Nobody knew who'd left it there. We got under the tarpaulin, but it didn't have any guns. The Head told us to keep away, but we played in it regularly. It was used by the Home Guard at nights.

My father was in the Home Guard. They guarded the main road south, at Kainies Crossing. There was a smithy with a gun-slit in the wall, under the blacksmith's furnace. They had to put the furnace out, before they could put the gun in. The gun was a smooth-bored thing called a Blacker Bombard – a mortar, only aimed horizontally. It was supposed to throw bombs at tanks.

In front, the first line of defence was a pillbox full of riflemen, and a row of round blocks of concrete, that could be rolled into the road, then up-ended to block it. Then someone had the bright idea of stopping the Germans by pouring petrol on the road and setting it alight. They got hold of a twenty-five gallon drum of petrol, and thought they'd try it. They poured the lot on the road and put a match to it. Unfortunately the flaming petrol ran down the drains, and out into the Burdiehouse Burn, and down it, floating on the water, still alight. I remember the line of fire, spreading, spreading, as fast as the burn ran, setting fire to the fields and trees. They had to call the fire brigade out.

It was very dark walking home from school in the blackout – in Scotland it got dark at three o'clock. One night I saw an enormous soldier walking along in green-grey overcoat and funny pointed cap. I followed him a long way. Then he heard my footsteps behind him. He whirled round and drew a Luger pistol from a big leather holster and pointed it straight at me. When he saw it was only a child, he burst out laughing uproariously. I was terrified. He was a Pole.

Just behind our house were the Braid Hills. There were two sledge-runs up there, we called the Cresta and the Livershaker. That winter, going up past the golf course, we noticed it had been wired-off, but not very well, not enough to stop us. On the golf course were two Spitfires and a hangar. But when we got up to them, the Spitfires weren't real, just full-size models made of plywood, just the tops of the wings and a body hollow underneath. The hangar was also a fake, just an empty Nissen hut. It was a fake airfield, built to deceive the German bombers from the air. We used to swing about inside the Spitfires, and camp inside them in the summer. We didn't think they were good enough to fool anybody.

Very early days. Rifles have replaced the pitchforks and shotguns, but there are no uniforms, few tin hats, and the 'armoured car' is an amateur job: workers at a jam factory have covered a Morris saloon with boiler-plate to make their own armoured car.

We didn't have many raids – only spent one night in the Anderson shelter. The Germans tried to hit the Forth Bridge, but all they got was Willy Younger's whisky distilleries at the bottom of Canongate. I remember the flashes from the Bofors guns, banging away on the bridge. Also the incredible blaze of the burning whisky, like an oil-refinery going up. People were lying in the gutters, drinking the whisky – the fire brigade couldn't get past for the bodies. Next day in Edinburgh there were thousands of drunks.

I saw one dogfight between a Hurricane and an Me 109 – over the Pentland Hills. We heard the guns firing, far away. Then smoke came out of the Messerschmitt, and it vanished over the hills and we heard the bang.

As we got older, we explored further and further. The firing-range on Alnwick Hall Road, from the 1914–18 war, still being used. We spent a lot of time collecting empty cartridge cases and stray bullets. Kids would pay you 1d. for the bullets, but the cartridge clips from the magazine fetched 3d. Better still were the ranges behind Dreghorn Castle. They used 2″ and 3″ mortars there. We used to search for bomb fins and the odd unexploded mortar bomb. When we found one we used to lug bricks at it, and occasionally we got one to explode. A bit dicey – they had a killing-range of 24 yards. One kid got killed picking up bombs and taking them home. Once they'd been fired they were fused, and if you turned them upside-down, the ball-bearing dropped down the tube and . . . wham!

Best of all were the mobile ranges at Glencarse. A circular railway track, with little bogies pulled on a chain by an engine. The soldiers arranged themselves so they could fire through the bogies into the bankside. The bogies carried plywood cut-outs of German soldiers, with helmets and grey uniforms, larger than life. As the bogies went round and round, the targets went up and down. There were target-tanks too, but the soldiers only used rifles, pistols and sten-guns.

The best place was the POW camp for German prisoners. But they weren't Germans, they were Ukrainians, who'd fought for the German army against Russia, then run away from the Russians to the West. They wore shit-brown denims with big green or orange circles on the back, and German peaked forage-caps or little circular caps. They worked on the farms during the day, short thick-set Slavs with broad cheekbones.

There were a hundred huts, surrounded by a big barbed-wire fence and watchtowers. Outside, there were trip-wires in the long grass, and barrel hoops honed razor sharp, that shot upright as you stepped on them. We used to get through the wire at night, to take the POWs fags and fish and chips. The guards were watching for POWs trying to get out, not kids trying to get in.

They were so glad to see children – used to take us into their huts. It could have been very dangerous, I suppose. But they made toys for us, model boats and tanks, really beautiful. And Russian-style tommy-guns with round magazines, not like ours. They used to stain them brown with tea or coffee – the stain came off on your hands when they got wet in the rain.

(After the war they were all shipped back to Russia against their wishes, and the Russians shot them.)

In January 1942, my father got his call-up papers – a buff envelope dropped on the doormat. Father was locked in the bathroom at the time, shaving. Mother told me to take it up and slip it under the bathroom door. That was the first time I ever heard my father swear. He swore continuously for a *very* long time.

We could always tell when we wakened up in the morning that my father had come home on leave – that lovely smell of khaki and boot-polish and gun-oil. He used to bring us home Service-issue boiled sweets from his compo-rations. All the soldiers did. Then they used to tell the Quartermaster that they'd lost them, and indent for more. They were the only sweets we saw in the war.

We roamed the fields unchecked, because there were hardly any farmworkers left. One of the few was an Irish horse-man called Joe McKean. He had no top-teeth, which together with his Irish accent made him hard to understand. He had eleven kids and a cottage with two rooms. The kids started off in the living-room, sleeping in apple-boxes, then graduated to orange-boxes, then went into the bedroom where they all slept in the family bed, top-to-tail. They were visited by the Catholic priest every week, till the eldest son produced a child by the eldest daughter ...

The other famous character was Sandy Shanky. His real name was Sandy Crawford. He was called 'Shanky' because he supplied Shanks toilets to army bases. He always drove round a lorry full of toilets. All through the war, his lorry got bigger and bigger, because he built on the back of it. By the end, there was nearly as much lorry behind the rear wheels as there was in front. After the war, he bought a great big garage over at Gilmerton.

My mother took us down to London for the wedding of my uncle, who was a parts-pusher – a man who went up and down the country finding out why deliveries of small parts for Spitfires were late, and holding up production. He would get them moving again. We went down to London by train. We had to stand all the way – twelve hours. A soldier gave my mother his seat, then tried to pick her up. After the wedding, my uncle took us round London. Cannon Street station was flat. High Holborn church was just a hole in the ground, with a single bell lying where the tower had been. But all the ruins were covered with the plant that Londoners called 'Bombsite' – rose bay willow-herb. My grandparents' house had had its back blown in twice – the back was just plywood, with no windows in the bedrooms – you had to have the light on all the time. All the streets were blocked with huge brick air-raid shelters, half-buried underground.

Boy, aged six to eight

1941 WAR IN THE LANCASHIRE COUNTRYSIDE

Me and my brother went across to the aerodrome next to our farm. It was nighttime and we both got over the fence. We then found an old bomber and got inside. With a hacksaw we had we cut out a giant fuel-tank. We had a struggle taking it back home, but when we got it home we hid it. The next morning we got it and cut the top off it. This we put on to the pond at the back of the haystacks and used it as a boat.

My sister Mary used to go to a man she knew who had an orchard. He let her take as many apples as she liked. She would make a stall outside our house and sell all the apples and pears. The money she made she would send to a fund to buy a bomber.

Joe Beacroft who owned Hooker's farm was once walking in the farmyard when he heard a plane coming. He ran into his house and went down the cellar. When the all-clear went, he got outside and looked round. He went past a fence and saw a hole about the depth of a pillar-box. A bomb was at the bottom. He then called someone to come and dispose it. But before they got there, it started to snow. It got so deep Mr Beacroft could not find where the hole was. The next minute he fell into the hole right up to his neck.

He soon got out!

Boy, aged fourteen

CHRISTMAS 1941

I woke early, my brother was asleep, so I made sure the blackout curtains were over the windows, and with my torch I had a little peep at my presents. I had a pair of slacks (Mummy made them out of a blanket) a paint-book, a pencil-box, and a very nice handkerchief, a book of poetry from Mummy, a bar of chocolate, a whole orange.

I have a very nice present for Mummy, I made it myself, a kettle-holder. And a present for Daddy, I made it, it is a case with needles and cottons and buttons in, so when he goes away he can sew his buttons on. I also made him a shoe-polisher. We had a lovely breakfast, fried bread and a nice egg. We're both very lucky, Richard and me, because Mummy and Daddy don't care much for eggs, or sweets.

Girl, aged 10. From Norman Longmate, How We Lived Then, *Hutchinson, 1971*

My daughter had asked Father Christmas for a doll's house. We looked at each other in dismay. Then my brother found an old bird-cage. During the raids he worked on it; found bits of cardboard for the walls. The office waste-paper basket provided an old file which made the roof. He painted the floors. We hunted for all kinds of bits and pieces and a miracle was achieved ... a piece of hessian, dyed red, fringed, made an elegant carpet. Never will I forget her face that dark Christmas morning and her childish voice piping 'There'll be bluebirds over the white cliffs of Dover' as she saw those tables and chairs, tiny pictures made from cigarette cards, her cries of joy as she discovered each new thing.

From Norman Longmate, How We Lived Then *(Hutchinson, 1971)*

WINTER
1942–3 NUISANCE RAIDS

The nuisance raids were the worst. Single bombers, only dropping a few bombs, but the siren would get you out of a warm bed into an ice-cold shelter two or three times a night. The first time we'd be well organized, folded blankets and thermos flasks; but by the third time people would be tripping over armfuls of bedding trailing along the wet ground, little kids bawling, getting slapped, couples screaming at each other, not from fear but because they were totally disorganized. You got punch-drunk, half-asleep, half-awake, day and night. All except our Norwegian neighbour, John Asmussen, a trawlerman. He used to come to our shelter, to see if we were all right; always gentle, cheerful, singing songs. Except he'd be sitting there and you'd suddenly realize he'd gone to sleep sitting up, still wearing his tin hat. He could sleep for five minutes whenever he wanted to, like a cat, and wake up better for it. Mam said it was him being in the trawlers; he'd learnt to snatch sleep between hauling in the nets, night-fishing.

One night, after he'd gone, I fell asleep in the bottom bunk of our shelter. I wakened in pitch darkness. The tiny oil-lamp above my head seemed to have gone out. I peered round, and couldn't see any red glow on the curved metal ceiling, from the candle in a flowerpot which was our only means of heating. I listened for the reassuring sound of my mother's breathing in the bunk above. Total silence. No sound from Brian Spedding, who slept opposite, only two feet away, or his Mam above. Just silence and pitch darkness.

I called; no answer. A bomb had killed them all, while I was asleep. There was no trickle of dim blue light round the shelter door-curtain . . .

I was buried alive! In blind panic I rolled out of my bunk on to the floor – that was the way I always did it – the bunk was only six inches off the shelter floor. I was screaming my head off.

Instead of falling six inches, I fell two feet, with a hell of a thump. On to carpet, not bare earth. The world was *insane*.

Then the light banged on, and Mam was standing there in her dressing-gown. I was in my own blacked-out bedroom. She told me the all-clear had gone hours ago, and I'd walked back from the shelter when she told me to, and got into bed.

I had walked in my sleep.

Boy, aged thirteen, Tyneside

1943 THE BIG BANG

Everybody around Northwich believed that if a German bomb hit ICI the whole of the town of Northwich would explode, and vanish. One day in 1943, the roof blew off the ICI prototype polythene plant. We got quite used to that in later years, but then everyone went rushing in to see how Northwich had vanished. We were quite disappointed to see everything was quite normal.

Girl, aged fifteen, Cheshire

CHAPTER 10 # THE WAR ON MERSEYSIDE

ON THE TRAMS

My Mum worked on the trams, as a conductor on the Pierhead to Woolton line. When she was on the afternoon shift, me and my sister used to go to the top of our road and get on the tram and go to Woolton Park for nothing. We would play in the park whilst the tram would turn round and have a tea-break, then we'd get back on and go home without paying.

STRANGE MEETING

It was very strange in the war. I had five children and every so often they would be out very late and I would ask why and they would say they were playing in the bombed-down church, and I would believe them. One night my neighbour came home and was quite concerned for my children. She said they were talking to a strange man. So I rushed down to the church, and there was my husband talking to my children.

But he was dead, months ago, I thought.

Then suddenly both the children and my husband had gone.

When I arrived back home, there were my children playing.

So I said nothing.

In the cramped terraced streets of Merseyside there was no room for Anderson shelters. Large brick surface shelters were a source of many casualties and much scandal. Some were left roofless, some built without cement.

ENCOUNTER IN THE DARK

Outside the houses they had things called pig-swills, that was every ten yards or so on the pavement, where people put all their orange peel if they got any, potato peel, etc.

My sisters, brothers and I were all going out to a dance, but they had gone on a little bit, so I had to follow on my own and you had to go up a dark street.

So my mum and dad gave me a torch and said 'If anyone creeps up behind you, shine the torch in their eyes, kick them your hardest and run.'

So I took the torch and was walking down the dark lane when I heard footsteps behind me. So I turned on the torch and shone it in the person's eyes ...

It blinded him for a few seconds and he fell in one of the pig-swills. He staggered up and had orange peel and all sorts of rubbish on his hat and over his coat. So I took to my heels and ran all the way to the dance.

When I got home my mother said 'Eeh, don't let your father know it was you shone the torch in his eyes, because he has got his new hat spoiled and his temper's foul.'

I didn't recognize my dad because it was a cold night and he had his hat down over his eyes and his coat pulled up round his ears.

Girl, aged sixteen

JUST IN TIME

I remember going to a dance, and on the way home I was stopped at a checkpoint for my identity card, but I couldn't find it. I was very worried by now because if you couldn't prove your identity you were put in prison till you could. So they took me back along the road looking for it. But then someone came running towards the checkpoint waving something in his hand and shouting at the top of his voice. It was the man I had been dancing with, and I had dropped my identity card while dancing, and he had run all the way in case I got stopped.

Girl, aged fifteen

POSTCARDS HOME

Our neighbour, Arthur Logan, was in the Air Force. His wife Mary Logan thought he was in the Navy because she was scared stiff of him being up in the air.

When he went to a different country (which was very often) he would always send his wife Mary a postcard with a ship on the front of it. This convinced her he was in the Navy. He never told her he was in the Air Force until the war had ended.

There were always two wars for the poor of Merseyside. One against the Jerries; the other a never-ending battle against poverty.

On one occasion he was stationed in the Far East and writing another postcard to Mary Logan when he was supposed to fly out on another routine flight. So somebody else took his place. The plane had been out a few hours, and another plane went out to see where it was, and they found it in pieces and all the crew were dead. From that day on he thought it was a miracle that another navigator took his place in the plane that crashed, while he was writing a postcard to his wife Mary Logan.

Boy, aged thirteen

WAR BABY

My Mum lived through the war by herself with my Dad at war for five years. Then my Mum had a baby in the last two years of the war. Sheilagh was the baby's name. In a newspaper my Mum's photograph was taken and underneath it said 'This little girl is waiting for her Dad to come home from the War.' And it was published!

A LIVELY GIRL

One day, during the war, I wanted to join the ARP, so I stayed out all night helping with the air raids. When I arrived home my mother battered me for staying out all night.

Another time I wanted to join the WRNS but my Mum wouldn't let me. Then I wanted to join the Army with my friend, and get posted to different countries. But when I saw the uniform, I didn't want to join because I didn't like the colour of the stockings. They were a horrible green colour. But my friend joined and got posted to Canada, and there she met a Canadian and lived there.

Girl, aged seventeen

CINEMA

During the war, you could get into a film free if you brought three jam jars. (The Film Company sold the jars back to the Jam Company.) This idea was fantastic, because every jar collected was kept in a yard at the back, and we used to sneak them out and use them again.

Boy, aged seven

SUSPENSE

One day during the war my Mum went out. My Dad was dead so there was no one to look after us, so my Mum shut us in the bedroom. I got really fed-up and wanted to go out and play. So I told my sister I would get out of the window and climb down the drainpipe, get in the back door and let her out. But when I tried to get out I slipped. Luckily my braces got caught on the window latch. I couldn't move so I had to wait there until my Mum came back. She then got the man next door to go up a ladder and get me down.

Boy, aged eleven

1942 DIRECT HIT

One of the greatest thrills was to travel on the ferry. Every second Sunday, my mother and I used to travel across to visit my grandmother who lived in New Ferry. The ferry would weave its way between large cargo-boats with guns and tanks on the decks and sometimes soldiers on board, all coming from America and Canada. Sometimes, because of the air raids on the river, we had to travel on the underground which went under the Mersey. Returning, we used to see people settling for the night on the platform of James Street Station – people who lived in the city centre, who felt safer in this large natural underground shelter. On one occasion the station received a direct hit from a bomb and was completely destroyed. I remember going through the station in the train a few days later. The exits from the platforms were blocked with bricks and debris. The station remained like that for the rest of the war.

1941 LANDMINE

There was a parachute and a landmine. The parachute was stuck on the school railings and a man pulled the parachute and the school blew up to pieces and so did the man.

Girl, aged six

1941 GETTING WHAT YOU ASK FOR

I'll never forget the night a group of dockers yelled back at some German bombers during a raid on Birkenhead. I worked on the cranes at the docks. One night the siren went off, we all ran to the shelter but it was full of water. So we dived beneath some railway wagons. This was no good. So we just stood in the avenue urging the Germans to try and hit us.

They did! A bomb landed on the other side of the dock – Victoria Dock – but luckily I wasn't hurt badly.

Boy, aged fifteen

MISSING PRESUMED KILLED

One of my cousins, Jackie, was reported 'missing presumed killed'. However, nearly two years later he just arrived out of the blue. Apparently he had been transferred from the ship he was on because he caught measles, but the next day the ship had been torpedoed and all hands drowned . . .

SAFE AND SOUND

In 1940 my brother Jim was reported missing in action. Sometime later he was reported dead.

A year later my eldest brother Frank was reported captured somewhere in Europe. He was then put in a prisoner-of-war camp in Germany. From there he wrote to say he had found his brother Jim, and that they were both safe and sound.

Boy, aged seven

1939   FROM THE DEAD

In 1939, my Dad worked on the Shell Jetty at the Dingle. They used to fill great barrels full of oil and load them on to a barge. They would be floated down the river, and loaded on to oil tankers. One night there was a huge explosion and the whole river was an inferno. My Dad and everyone else on the barge had to dive in the river and swim for the shore. Quite a few men died that night, but my Dad was lucky. He escaped with burns and his back looked like a map.

DEC
1941   THE BOMBERS' MISTAKE

My mother and I were sleeping peacefully when we were awoken suddenly by a large explosion, which came from German bombers who were bombing what they thought was Liverpool, but in fact was an RAF camp being built around the clock at Meols, near Hoylake. Wave after wave of bombers flew by; realizing their mistake, they flew on towards Liverpool. My mother and I spent the whole night under the Morison in the lounge with our neighbour Mrs Sadler and her daughter Susan, singing and sometimes praying and sometimes saying the Rosary as the noise of the bombers came near our house. In the morning you could see the smoke of fires coming from the camp. After that night, Susan and I were evacuated to stay with relatives in Wales.

Girl, aged thirteen

1941   NEW GAMES

We used to play a game where you used the bricks off wrecked houses and you had to build a little base big enough for yourself to get in. They called this game the Shelter Game. This was not the only game they played with bricks; they also played a game where you had to balance as many bricks as you could on top of each other.

Girl, aged fifteen

ACK-ACK GUNS

I still remember the street I used to live in – Balan Street. Forty-two light Ack-ack lived there too. Every so often in the middle of the night the searchlights would go on, and a gun towed behind a truck would pull up right outside my house and start firing. The noise was deafening, and off the guns came a lot of smoke that made you cough. Also where the truck stopped and the gun was set up there was a big indentation in the ground which came from all the used shells dropping out of the gun on to the road causing this ditch-like thing.

Boy, aged ten

GRANDA

Granda, during the Blitz, always went around with about twenty felt hats on his head, to keep the bombs off. One night he was walking home with eggs in his pockets. The siren went but he kept on walking until the bombs came whizzing down so he dived for cover and suddenly realized he'd smashed the eggs . . . We lived at 38 Mighall Street. Granda didn't like Mr Scott who lived next door at No. 36. One night an incendiary bomb landed in our yard. It did not explode and Granda went out and the bomb had the number 36 on it. 'There y'are,' said Granda, 'I knew it was meant for him next door,' and he threw the bomb into 36's yard, but it never went off.

Boy, aged ten

1939–40 JOEBOE

Joeboe was the youngest of ten children. When war started he had to be evacuated to Wales. But when the time came he didn't want to go, he didn't want to leave his mother Mary (called Dolly) and he done nothing but cry – he was only eleven and it was the first time he was away from the family. When the day came he went missing for a couple of hours and all the family had to go and look for him. When they found him he had to go and get a bus for Wales. Winifred took him because he was very attached to her.

Joeboe hated his new home. When his only friend Steve ran away, the elderly couple sent for Winifred. Joeboe told Winifred to ask the bus driver to try to find Steve. For hours they drive around and in the end Steve was found by a lane and they all went back to Liverpool.

Joeboe went back to a desolate wrecked jungle. Churches were rubble and houses were bits of brick and wood. Joeboe bought a bike for half-a-crown and he would ride round blitzed Liverpool for hours. One day Joeboe left his bike at a friend's house. The house was bombed and Joeboe's rusty bike was found wrecked. His family thought he was dead.

'Me boy, me boy,' cried Mary Dunn. 'He's dead.'

But Joeboe had taken his time coming home. When he did arrive home, Mary thought it was a miracle and that he'd come back from the dead.

Joeboe said 'I seen the bomb coming down, so I ducked behind a wall and the bomb hit the bike.' Mary thought it was his guardian angel had saved him, and James Dunn was very proud of his quick thinking until the truth came out he'd been nowhere near the bomb, then Joeboe was battered. Joeboe was a talented boy who taught himself to play the piano and he played it well. He could tell a scary tale, and he used to sing for money round the air-raid shelters.

1941   BEHIND THE DUST-CART

When the siren went, I always let my dog 'Size Nine' out, because when that dog heard the siren he seemed to have a sudden urge to do his duty. Some nights I had to go out looking for Size Nine, because he did not come back. I always found him hiding behind the old dust-cart that my grandad used to use.

'THERE WAS NO HOME'

When morning came we left the shelter and made our way home. There was no home. All that was left was a pile of bricks. We had nowhere to live except the shelter, and that was to be our home for six months. We had our meals at different relations'.

144

BRINGING THE DEAD OUT

There were big houses at the back of us which were practically demolished. There were only odd walls standing, and as they were bringing the dead out they were put in bags then in large bins. It was very frightening.

Girl, aged eighteen

'There was no home.' Four-month-old Dorothy was born in a Blitz, and is here seen in the arms of her grandmother after their home had been destroyed.

1941 GOODBYE, GRANDAD

One day, 4 May 1941, the day after the heaviest bombing in Liverpool, my Mum went out to see if her Mum was all right. When she came back she seen a hole in the wall opposite her house. She came in and told my Grandad.

He went out to look at it. While he was out, a bomb went off. He did not come back and my Gran thought he had gone to see if his Mum was all right. After one hour she went to his mother's but he wasn't there. She came back with my Uncle Tom and told him about the hole. He found the building with the hole was on fire, and the local soldiers, the King's Liverpool Regiment, was there.

My Uncle Tom told them the story about the hole. When the fire was under control and was almost out, the soldiers began to dig away the rubble. They found my Grandad, and lying next to him was a policeman. My Uncle Tom said 'He must have gone for a policeman, then the bomb went off.' It was a time-bomb, and the watchman was not there.

Girl, aged twelve

GOODBYE, MUM

As I queued up in a very long line, the siren went. The queue dispersed very quickly and I and many others fled to the nearest shelter in Blackstock Square. As I entered I looked round for my father and mother. My father was there but my mother was not. Everyone said they hadn't seen her. I began to get very worried but my father comforted me.

When the all-clear went, off we went back home. But my mother could not be seen. I entered the house and began to cook two sausages. My father walked in the house as white as a sheet.

'Your mother is dead!' he spluttered. I didn't know what to do. I just broke down and cried and cried and cried, for a good half an hour. My father tried to comfort me but it was no good. It was very hard getting over her death, but I will never forget that terrible day.

1942 A NIGHT TO REMEMBER

My mother used to play Bingo every Tuesday night at the Church Social with her friend Moira, who was married to an Australian sailor. He knew my father was in the Merchant Navy, on a ship called the SS *Rag-Brittan*. He also heard on the news that she had been torpedoed with great loss of life. Fearing the worst, he wanted his wife to comfort my mother in case my father was one of the casualties. That night at the Bingo, the women couldn't stop winning, and the following day my father arrived home in an ambulance. My mother knew there was something wrong that night, but had a feeling my Dad was all right. She said she had a premonition something had happened.

Girl, aged twelve

NOT MUCH USE

On the way home from a dance with my brothers and sisters, the siren went. We were quite a way from home, so we ran into this square, where Tommy, the eldest, saw an air-raid shelter. So we all ran into it. Bombs and machine-guns filled the air. Everybody was scared stiff, so we huddled together with our eyes shut, to seek comfort from each other. Then Peggy looked up and said, 'D'you want to know something? But ... erm ... this shelter hasn't got a roof on it.' Everybody looked up, and Tommy said 'Run home, quick.' It was about half a mile and all the girls were crying, but to make matters worse we were running through an air raid.

At home we all dived down the shelter, then after a cup of tea Dad said 'Right, where was that shelter? I'm going down tomorrow to see that bloody council. These shelters are a bloody disgrace. They'd better do something about them, or else.'

Girl, aged sixteen

LITTLE MOTHER

There were nine children, including myself. In the war it was very difficult for me, because my sister and me and my mum had to look after the other children. I was very poor, and hopeless at school because I hardly ever went, because I had to see to the children. I had no friends because I had no time to make any. I loved my family but most of the time I wished I was an only child, because in school I was the lowest in my class and everybody said I was thick and lazy. I had no time to revise for exams, and hardly never done homework. My life was babies, babies and more babies.

Girl, aged thirteen

C.B. 4/10

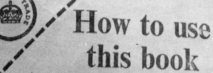

How to use this book

1. This Clothing Book must be detached immediately from the Food Ration Book (see page I); and the holder's name, full postal address and National Registration number written in the spaces provided on page I in INK.

2. All the coupons in this book do not become valid at once. IT IS ILLEGAL TO USE ANY COUPON UNTIL IT HAS BEEN DECLARED VALID.

3. When shopping, you must not cut out the coupons yourself, but must hand this book to the shopkeeper and let him cut them out. IT IS ILLEGAL FOR THE SHOPKEEPER TO ACCEPT LOOSE COUPONS.

4. When ordering goods by post, do not send this book—cut the coupons out, and send them with your order BY REGISTERED POST.

5. If you join one of the Services take this book with you; it will be asked for. The Clothing Books of deceased persons must be handed to the Registrar of Births and Deaths when the death is notified.

6. This book is the property of H.M. Government and may only be used by or on behalf of the person for whom it is issued. TAKE GREAT CARE NOT TO LOSE IT.

S.Q. 48. 16/11/48. £88

PAGE II

PAGE V

CHAPTER 11 **FOOD**

SOME BLOODY FUNNY THINGS

We never starved, but we ate some bloody funny things. Best was American dried egg. You poured a thin trickle into the frying-pan, then as it cooked it blew up like a balloon, till it was two inches thick, like a big yellow hump-backed whale.

And we had whale meat, that tasted strongly of fish, unless you soaked it for twenty-four hours in vinegar, after which it tasted of vinegar. But there was so much of it – great big bloody steaks as big as your plate – that we didn't care what it tasted like.

Sausage-meat was pale pink – I don't think it had any meat in it at all. Late in the war, my mother got a pound of 'butcher's sausage' – the sausage a butcher made for his own family. It seemed indecent, cos lumps of real meat kept dropping out of it – it nearly made us sick.

I lived a lot on chip-butties – but you had to eat them quick, before the chips turned dark blue.

The government posters made us all hate the 'Black Market' – though no one ever knew what a 'Black Marketeer' looked like. But all through the war, things kept 'appearing' in our house. One Christmas, a whole unopened box of Mars Bars. Another time, a seven-pound tin of butter, which for some reason we kept in the bath. I enjoyed carving great caves out of it. When I asked Dad where these things came from, he'd say 'bought it off a feller at work' or 'off the ships', so matter-of-factly that it never occurred to me till after the war that my father must have 'received goods knowing them to have been stolen' – from the Black Market.

Luckily, we had a neighbour on the trawlers. My parents

looked after his wife while he was at sea, especially when she was pregnant, so we were never short of fish. And we had a large greenhouse – immediately after every raid my father would go and check how many panes the Germans had blown out – by the end of the war, it wasn't so much a glasshouse as a cardboard-house, but all through we had so many tomatoes, we sold them to other people.

My mother spent our week's holiday in Cumberland collecting eggs from all the surrounding farms, a dozen at a time. At first she was treated with great suspicion, as a Ministry of Ag. and Fish snooper, but by the end of the war, she'd come home with twelve dozen in a carrier bag.

My friend Ally Johnson dropped his mother's carrier, containing twelve dozen eggs, in Newcastle Haymarket Bus Station, right under the nose of a policeman. He said the yellow egg yolk just spread and spread, all over the road; the Johnsons took to their heels.

In 1939, I was a thin child; by 1941, I was an enormous fat elephant. I think my mother saw fattening me up as a patriotic duty. Our dog got very fat as well. Our neighbour in the trawlers used to see it as a good-luck mascot – when he went on a trip, he used to always come and stroke our dog first. When he came back safe, he would give our dog a whole pound block of Cadbury's chocolate. The dog used to bring it home in its mouth, with half the wrapping chewed off; my mother would immediately requisition it. The number of times we handed round tooth-marked chocolate at Christmas . . .

My mother seemed to have no appetite in the war. She'd sit my father and I down to something tasty, then announce 'I'm not really hungry. I'll have my share later. I think I'll just have a little bit of bread and butter . . .'

Boy, Tyneside

WELCOME HOME

When people who'd been out at the war for a time returned to their home town, people put up banners saying 'Welcome home, Peter!'

Well, when rationing was on, mums had to queue for hours. One day, my mum was gone all day queuing for potatoes, and when she came home there was a big banner across the street saying 'Welcome home Mum', because she'd been gone all day for a couple of spuds.

Girl, Liverpool

Growing food was one way they would let us help: they turned our school playing-field into allotments. Unfortunately, it had recently been laid down on a levelled corporation rubbish tip. Once the turf was lifted, we found ourselves trying to plant cabbages, carrots and potatoes in soil composed of rusted tin cans, kipper bones and brown-edged copies of the Daily Express. I stole a lot of my dad's bonemeal – planted vegetables into solid pits of bonemeal. Everything grew amazingly well ... the family enjoyed everything. Dad never found out where his bonemeal had gone.

NOT ENOUGH RABBITS

One morning I went to the market to buy apples and I had to stand in a long queue in the cold morning air. When at last it was my turn to be served he gave me a pound of apples. As he was doing so I noticed he placed two bad apples in the pound I

had. So I told him that I didn't want them, and could he replace them? With that he took the bag of apples off me, gave me my money back and told me to go. I was very angry because the apples were not for me but for my children. I swore at him then I went away. When I arrived home my husband said 'If I'd been treated like that I'd have knocked his stall over and thrown his rotten fruit at him.'

A week later I went to the market again for some meat. On the meat stall was the same man again, selling rabbits. I stood in the queue hoping he would not recognize me because I knew if he did I would not get my rabbit. He started counting how many rabbits he had, so that them waiting would not be waiting for nothing. When he'd finished counting the rabbits he started to count us. When he came to me he said 'Sorry, love, not enough rabbits'. If he'd been lying I'd have tipped his stall over and thrown the rabbits at him like my husband said.

The queue was seen by some women as a misery, by some as essential war-work to beat Hitler, by some as a free social occasion. Some shopkeepers had more leeway than others, some were more susceptible to customer's charms. Dark allegations were made against shopkeepers' sexual morals (especially butchers!).

Local papers were not allowed to write about their local war for fear of helping German Intelligence. No doubt smuggled-out pictures of these block-buster marrows, grown in Paignton, Devon, must have made Adolf's heart sink . . .

CIGARETTES

When me and my sister were about nine and eleven years old, my Dad used to smoke Winston cigarettes. So every morning about five our Dad woke us up. There were two tobacconists. So one of us went in one queue, and the other in the other queue. When we got the cigarettes we swopped queues to get some more. We done this every morning for two years, every morning except Sunday.

Girl, aged nine, Liverpool

RATIONS

I hated everything being on ration. In the morning we used to get up and my Mum used always to be making porridge. But because sugar was on ration it tasted horrible, and it tasted worse if you put salt on it. Then I remember Mum finding a tin of syrup in the cupboard and instead of having sugar on porridge we had syrup and it was delicious.

Girl, aged sixteen, Liverpool

The milkman often brought the first details of the night's bombing. I can never remember the milkman and his well-trained horse (which followed him and came to his whistle like a dog) failing to get through, however bad the bombing had been.

PIGS

Our family never went short of food. My uncle was a farmer. He used to breed pigs. He was allowed to kill so many pigs for himself, and the rest went to the government. So he used to kill one on the sly and give it to my Dad. They used to put the dead pig in the bath, to soak overnight. My aunty went to the toilet in the night and she saw the pig lying in the bloodstained water. She didn't know it was a pig and she let out a scream that woke everyone in the house.

Girl, aged fourteen, Liverpool

KEEP
A PIG

Join
or start
A PIG
CLUB

FOR ADVICE AND INFORMATION APPLY TO –
SMALL PIG KEEPERS' COUNCIL, VICTORIA HOUSE, SOUTHAMPTON ROW, W.C.1.

Nobody kept a pig round our way: the smell was too bad, the neighbours would have complained. But at one time, I had twenty-seven rabbits – a whole village of hutches. Then I lost interest and my mother had to feed them – toast and dandelion and baked potato-peelings. They died or vanished somewhere, one by one. We ate the last one – a buck called Big Lugs, a friend of four years' standing – for our Christmas dinner, 1944. I couldn't eat a bite. My father kept Big Lugs' tail for pollinating his tomatoes. In that tail was summed up all of guilt and mortality. The boys in the photograph, from Croydon, Surrey, were running their own rabbit farm.

SHORTAGES

As a young girl I loved to go to the dances. I only had two best dance dresses, which I had to alter every now and then to make them look different. We used to get some material or nice paper and fold it carefully to make belts.

We had an open coal fire, but coal was on ration. I can remember my Dad going into the woods and chopping down one of the trees so we could have wood for the fire. I thought it was great to see a tree being chopped. My Dad and brother spent all day chopping it up. I can remember my Dad with a wheelbarrow going round the neighbours giving out the logs.

I can remember the state our whole estate was in when the Co-op got a box of bananas. Everyone queued up for hours. My mam dragged me to the shop with her. Just one banana and we had to wait all day. I was really bored.

You could hardly get wool and so my Mum used to undo all my Dad's old jumpers to make us hat, gloves, wool socks and scarves; if she had enough wool, all to match. I used to be the envy of the street.

Sometimes the coal ration would run out, so we would put the gas oven on and put our feet inside to keep ourselves warm.

Nobody could afford to make a birthday cake, so instead you had a decorated hatbox as a cake, or a wooden cake with candles on.

Girl, aged sixteen

1941–2 BANANAS AND ONIONS

I had never saw or eaten a banana. Where I lived there was a prisoner-of-war camp behind us. One day I was walking to the shops when a prisoner called us to the fence and offered us three bananas (for my sister and my brother). Not knowing how to eat it we peeled the banana, ate the skin and threw the inner away.

When me and my sister and my brother and Mum were going to the shops for a few groceries at four o'clock, the sentries came out of that camp. All the lights were out and they came out with the customary words: 'Friend or foe?'

You had to step two paces forward and say 'Friend' and show your identity card. But ,on this particular evening my mother neglected to bring our identity cards (even I had one when I was five) so we were taken to the police station all night and morning. So we had to wait till Gran came with our cards.

My father, who was in the Royal Navy, would bring home three onions when he came on leave. He gave one to my grandmother, one to me mum and one to the priest. The priest would then, when he had the onions, put them in a raffle and make twenty pounds, which today would be 200 pounds, just for one onion.

We lived at Knowsley, but at Speke there was an ammunition factory, but we did not know it was an ammunition factory. We wondered why it was not bombed. Then we were told it was painted and camouflaged as a farm. Speke Hall was the farmhouse and Dunlop's ammunition factory was painted as a duck-pond with ducks on it.

We had a shop down our road; a blind lady was the proprietor. We used to put a piece of blotting-paper under the sweet-coupon page on the ration-book, and trace round it and cut out the blotting-paper in the shape of coupons. The old lady felt the texture and shape of the blotting-paper and was deceived into thinking it was the coupons and we took the sweets.

My father worked in the slaughterhouse before the war, and he made good friends. While father was away they used to send my mother half a lamb, pig, tripe, cowheels, pig's trotters etc., and my mother would swap them for jam, sugar or tea which were great luxuries.

GREEN VEGETABLES & SALADS help you to resist infection, clear the skin, and take the place of raw fruit.

Slowly the idea dawned that what you ate might actually affect your body. Before the war, we ate what was nice – fish and chips, sausages, pies, cakes, sweets – with hardly a green vegetable in sight. The Ministry of Food tried to popularize a cattle-food called 'curly-kale'. All I knew was that lettuce gave my rabbits fatal diarrhoea, so I never ate it.

don't forget
Jimmy's
orange juice &
cod liver oil

Only the really poor went for this stuff; it tasted yuk! However, I was bought a commercial brand of cod liver oil and malt, thick like treacle and tasting like toffee. And I was purged regularly with agonies called senna pops and Gregory powder, both of which seem thankfully to have vanished from the earth since.

When the Germans were occupying the prison camp through the woods, a gang of us would collect all the horse dung and throw the dung at the waiting Germans (Krauts).

As there was a great shortage of toys, we played top-and-whip with a lemonade screw-top and a shoelace. My brother had a train set made out of the handle of a brush that made the coaches and engine, and nailed-on pennies for wheels.

Once my uncle came home on twenty-four-hours leave. He had all his Army things. Once we got our hands on them, we soon had so many each of the bullets. But we started complaining on the amount we should have each, so my mother came in, in a rage. Not knowing what they were, she took them off us and threw them on the fire and said 'No one will have them.'

Then a sudden burst of gunfire broke out in our living-room, so we took cover behind the settee.

Girl, aged six

A potato-peeling party: the potato had a magical quality in the war. 'Woolton pie', named after the Minister of Food, was composed solely of potatoes and herbs, with a crust on top. Potato-peelings were kept, crisped in the oven, fed to rabbits, hens and pigs. We somehow felt that the potato was a secret weapon that would beat Hitler, even when (final disaster) they were rationed for a short time. We British had a gift of making desperation into parties.

1941 EMERGENCY RATIONS

Our school took Air Raid Practice very seriously. We had to assemble complete with gasmask, coat and 'emergency rations' and run down the road (in twos of course) to the shelter.

We were not, of course, allowed to eat our 'emergency rations'; they had to be kept for 'the real thing'.

I looked longingly at my 'emergency rations' from time to time. Inside the tin, which lived under my desk at all times, there was, I knew, a large 'Kit Kat', amongst other goodies rarely seen.

I did not, however, allow myself as much as a *nibble*. These might well be NEEDED. LATER ON! Our teacher insisted.

One day, when my rations had reposed in my desk, untouched for several weeks, I decided to check the contents for deterioration. Silas Marner could not have been more shocked. The tin was empty, my precious Kit Kat gone! In great distress I went straight to the teacher.

Her face turned bright red.

Girl, aged nine, Cheshire

1940 BUTTER IN THE BOOT

The Home Guard used our schoolyard to drill in. We regarded this schoolyard as ours – and them as trespassers. We used to peep over the wall at them drilling, and rag them. Some stupid members didn't know their left foot from their right. We used to shout out commands, left turn, right turn, while their sergeant was shouting them. In the end the sergeant would get so mad it became a chase-job . . .

They caused my grandfather great inconvenience, because all they ever seemed to do was set up checkpoints on the outskirts of Carmarthen town – a mass of sandbags that reduced the road to half-width, so they could stop every car and search it for spies and Fifth-columnists. My grandfather was neither – he was a farmer, and before the war he used to buy in butter from the other farmers and blend seventeen different kinds of butter. Now all his milk went to the Milk Marketing Board, and he didn't blend butter any more. But he still had plenty of contacts in the butter trade, and none of our family ever went short of butter. . . . He had an old Standard 9, with the boot under the back seat, and into that would go these pounds and pounds of butter, and off we'd go through the Carmarthen checkpoints with me sitting on top of it. A bit hair-raising, if they decide to search the car, in spite of the innocent child sitting in the back . . . we could've both gone to prison.

But my father's in the Carmarthen Home Guard as well . . .

Boy, aged eleven, Carmarthenshire

"Keep it under your hat!"

CARELESS TALK COSTS LIVES

CHAPTER 12 SPIES

1940 SPY!

The news on the wireless was a must. Each word of Alvar Liddell was savoured and recorded, not only for discussion with your peers, but to relate to your Dad on his return from the pit.

'The R A F have bombed Tobruk, Dad!'

'The Eyeties have been chased out of Sidi Barrani.'

Atlases were pored over; the disposition of troops, Allied and Axis, faithfully recorded. A broadcast announcing a victory, or even a partial success, was inevitably marked by the raising of a small Union Jack, a relic of the 1937 Coronation, on a tall garden cane affixed to the backyard gate. Anyone entering the back lane couldn't but be aware of the state of the nation in its historic conflict.

His Majesty's Government, in their wisdom, had told us that 'Walls have ears' and 'Look out – there's a spy about'. Wall-posters – by far the most fascinating to me was the Spy Poster. Depicted was a city gent in bowler, with brolly, striped trousers, black coat and carrying a briefcase. This person, we were confidently informed, could be a spy.

In a community used to its menfolk in coal-grimed work-clothes and blackened faces, the sight of such sartorial elegance was utterly alien. Even the doctor did not aspire to such heights!

We re-enacted the various battles on the piece of waste ground at the end of the colliery row. Small, nondescript, it became in turn the sands of North Africa, the Jungle of Burma, the Beach of Dunkirk. Dunkirk became a historic victory on our 'beach' – two valiant Britishers against the overwhelming odds of four 'Nazis' reluctantly recruited among our companions.

The Government was nearly as hysterical about German spies as about gas: in reality, the German spy network in England was late, amateurish and rather pathetic, as Hitler had never expected to invade Britain, until late 1940. Nevertheless, spy posters kept us cheerful by being witty.

The government followed our lead. Very soon, the ignominy which led to Dunkirk became, as we had already portrayed, the brilliantly organized evacuation which has been recorded in history.

The aftermath of the real Dunkirk was that the village was invaded by hundreds of troops to be billeted in the church and miner's halls. Trucks were deployed in nearby farmers' fields and – joy – *real* tanks rolled into the bed of the sand quarry. Our war-games took a secondary place as, encouraged by *real* soldiers, we joy-rided in bren-gun carriers and explored the depths and mysteries of the gun-turret of a real tank. The days were all too short; we had much to thank Hitler for.

It was about this time that our portrayal of the Siege of Tobruk (or was it the Ordered Withdrawal From Greece?) took place on the waste ground at the end of our street. Fighting had been heavy all morning, until our respective calls to dinner. Battle recommenced immediately thereafter with numerous casualties, and immediate resurrections, on both sides. Honours were about even, and calls of 'skinch' announced that this sector of the world conflict wanted a breather. Our makeshift rifles were set aside and we sank to the grassless earth.

'Who's he?' asked General (later Field Marshal) Erwin Rommel. The eyes of friend and foe alike were directed towards the bottom of the street. There, setting up a tripod on which was a 'telescope thing', was a man the like of whom had never been seen outside the wall-posters.

'Bowler hat?'

'Yes!'

'Black coat?'

'Yes!'

'Striped trousers?'

'Yes, yes!'

'And he's got spats too!' whispered a ten-year-old who only minutes before had been General Alexander. We watched curiously as the intruder set up his instrument and pointed it at the end of the row of houses. He peered into the eyepiece, made slight adjustments and peered again. Then he straightened up and reached for a leather satchel, nearby.

'A briefcase!' we whispered. Conclusive and damning. 'He's a spy!'

By this time the spy had taken from his briefcase a notebook and pencil and, after more peering and adjusting, wrote down what were undoubtedly facts of vital importance to the outcome of the war relative to a row of colliery houses. The spy and his equipment now moved nearer our battlefield.

'Shall we capture him?'

'He's a big feller, mind!'

General Rommel, temporarily retired but still with the astuteness of his recent role, suggested 'Let's tell PC Wilson!'

Some, mainly those who had recently been 'Germans', were in favour of tackling the spy and taking him by force. Already they were brandishing their broomstick rifles. Good sense and generalship prevailed, and we agreed to inform PC Wilson, who lived in a neighbouring street. Our main force would make its way the long way round. To allay suspicion, two of our force would need to make their way past the spy. They could, if opportunity arose, gather more damning evidence as they passed him. Two dirty-faced, sweaty, khaki-shorted, sand-shoed troopers made their tentative way down the lane. Step by step they neared the bowler-hatted man, who continued to devote his attention to the lens of his theodolite. Young Denis was tempted to blurt out 'Are you a spy?' as they got abreast of him. Alan, proud of his meagre knowledge of German, thought of astounding the Nazi by shouting 'Achtung! Achtung!'

That might allow him to escape though, and neither uttered a sound as they passed.

PC Wilson was standing in his shirt-sleeves at his back door, listening to the other boys, his face impassive as he towered above and listened to the motley band of erstwhile warriors.

'A spy, eh? Well, let's see then!' The group stood to one side, as he donned his police jacket and peaked hat, en route to the backyard gate. The strange procession began its trek. Perhaps a little pity developed in all of us for the spy. All of us had experienced the wrath of PC Wilson; his cuff about the ear for minor, and his heavy service boot in the rear for major, misdemeanours were well known and respected.

Then our mothers appeared, as if by evil magic, at back doors.

'Alan, come here this minute!'

'Your tea's been on the table for ages, our Billy!'

'TOMMY!'

'Ah, Mam, just a couple of minutes . . .'

All pleas went unheeded. PC Wilson alone turned the corner to confront the representative of Hitler's Germany.

Teas were hurriedly downed, and chores done with hitherto unknown alacrity. Once free, the group raced down the street, rounded the corner to the scene of the 'capture'.

Deserted. No policeman, no spy, nothing!

'Mr Wilson will have handcuffed him and taken him to prison.'

'Probably has him locked up in his coalhouse.'

'He'll be int . . . introg . . . questioning him.'

'The Army looks after all spies because they have bullets and guns to shoot them.'

So the speculation went until dusk and our maternally imposed curfew. The six o'clock news was listened to with great anticipation ... When nothing materialized, we gave an enigmatic hint to our parents to be sure to call us should PC Wilson call, or should there be any particular item on the nine o'clock bulletin after we'd gone to bed ...

When we gathered on subsequent days, we agreed that no news is good news. National Security was the reason our exploit could not be publicized.

'They won't want old Hitler to know he's been captured.'

Our 'Hallo, Mr Wilson,' when we met our fellow spy-catcher in the street met with, disappointingly, only a smile, a pat on the head and a cautionary 'Now don't get into any mischief, boys.'

Jimmy the postman was closely watched and followed, in case he omitted to deliver any official-looking letters to our homes.

'Surely Mr Churchill will write. Or mention us in one of his speeches.' He had mentioned one 'Few', and we had been even fewer.

Boy, Tyneside

1940 A SPY AT ROEDEAN

Our headmistress was the sort you automatically placed in the category 'dragon'. Not the flame-breathing variety – worse. Cold and austere and you knew she would never lose her temper or shout, which at least would have made her human. Tilda was tall, and went straight down back and front without any bulges, so you couldn't even titter about her large bosom/fat wobbly bottom. She had grey cropped hair and a thin-lipped mouth. And taught Maths. That was *it*, as far as I was concerned. At nine, I couldn't do Maths and I was terrified of her.

We had to write down impossible numbers like five million, twenty-five thousand and two ... I could never get it right. I couldn't remember how many noughts ... The awful business of being called on to give an answer, mine inevitably being wrong. Our grand totals would be announced to everyone. If you got nought, you were never shouted at, only subjected to a look of withering scorn, so I wished a hole would appear in the floor.

However, life had its redeeming features. We all collected in Tilda's room and sat on the floor and were read to. Whole books from start to finish, in good big chunks and usually our choice,

Safe from a war they would much rather have joined in. The girls of Roedean, evacuated to Keswick for the duration, outside their temporary school hotel in 1941.

while we sat industriously knitting shapeless grey garments for the Troops. God knows what the Troops must have thought, when the parcels were unpacked in far-off POW camps – my first effort was a scarf that reached record proportions lengthwise, and zig-zagged in and out as I alternately acquired and lost stitches.

Sometimes I was asked to read aloud, when Tilda had a sore throat – Biggles books – I always thought girls' books were soppy, like *Little Women* and *Good Wives* and that ghastly *Anne of Green Gables*. Captain W.E. Johns wrote about *real* things happening *now*. Aeroplane dogfights – invasion by Germans – spies.

One day, in a fit of loathing for Tilda engendered by coming bottom in the Maths test again, I thought 'Perhaps *she* is a German spy?' She seemed quite horrid enough. I mentioned it to my friend Tony. She thought it a definite possibility. But how could we actually *prove* it, before writing to the authorities? Even Biggles had to act on proof. But, how?

Tony and I slept next to Tilda, high up on the third floor of the converted Keswick hotel that was our wartime school. The windows were dormers, with a nice piece of sloping roof below.

'Get into Tilda's room along the roof and search for evidence?' suggested Tony. Tony said she'd go first, while I kept a lookout.

"..... but of course it **mustn't** go **any** further!"

CARELESS TALK COSTS LIVES

Terribly funny ... The feet, we knew from long experience, belonged to Adolf and Fatty Goering, even though the faces were never drawn.

We chose one long summer's evening after lights-out, when it was impossible to lie in bed and just go to sleep. I positioned myself at the top of the stairs, and Tony opened the window and crept out on to the roof. After a few minutes she was back, all excitement.

'Just what we wanted,' she said. 'She has newly washed handkerchiefs stuck all over her window in a funny pattern. They are obviously a specially coded message for the ENEMY. The window's visible from the mountains, and another spy's only got to train his binoculars on Tilda's window ...'

166

Savage. Adolf is listening, but he is also dressed as a humble waiter, and lying on his belly on the floor.

TITTLE TATTLE LOST THE BATTLE

Of course, I had to see the Message. What did it mean? Troop movements? Invasion Imminent? The view from the high roof was marvellous, but I didn't like the feeling in my tummy when I looked down at the ground. It seemed a long way below.

I scrambled back into our bedroom.

Footsteps coming upstairs . . .

Tilda, of course. 'Now, Antonia and Elizabeth, just what are you doing?' The voice was icy with suppressed fury. 'I think you'd better come to my room and explain . . .'

Girl, aged nine

WHATEVER'S IN HIS POCKETS,
YOU MAY WANT IT,
INTELLIGENCE NEED IT !
HAND IT OVER

This poster at least was based on reality: anything or anyone descending from the sky was stripped bare unless instantly and closely guarded. We had an unslakeable thirst for souvenirs.

1941 CATCH 'EM YOUNG

A lad I was at school with was, as a fourteen-year-old, approached by MI6. He'd returned to England in 1939 because his German mother had just died (his English father was already dead), to live with his uncle. He was quizzed as to his life in Germany and was told they would 'be in touch' and was asked if he would be 'willing to return to Germany' one day. He did, in 1945, as an NCO interpreter with the Intelligence Corps.

Boy, aged fourteen, County Durham

1941 SPIES?

One night, about 2.30 a.m., the siren sounded. Dad shouted up: 'Come on, girls, wrap up and get down the shelter.'

DONT TELL
AUNTY & UNCLE
OR COUSIN JANE
AND CERTAINLY NOT ——

G. LACOSTE

The Ministry of Home Security at its silliest. Not a single German spy was found to be female, let alone beautiful, by the time the whole British network was rolled up in 1944. Neutral ports were perhaps different: one British sailor was shot as a traitor after giving information about the movements of his own ship to a Portuguese dance-hostess.

I said to Margaret 'Tell Dad I'm fast asleep.' Margaret went down and I crept out of bed and had a look out of the window.

I saw something, and shouted to Dad to come up and have a look. So up came Dad and said 'Come down to the shelter,' but I said 'No, Dad, look out of the window.'

So Dad took a look and said 'Hey, love, you're right! Keep an eye on them while I phone the police.'

Soon three policemen were looking out of our bedroom window, across the street to a house with a big french window. Then, as the police were going to investigate we heard an almighty crash. The crash was the french window being smashed by Dad; he took an almighty piece of coal and hurled it through the window and came back saying 'There, that'll teach the buggers.'

What was it I had saw? Well, in that house there were people moving about, with all the lights out, so they were silhouetted against the moonlight, and they were all wearing tin helmets so they reflected the moon's rays and I thought they were spies sending messages to each other by code, because every time they moved their heads, the moonlight caught them.

Girl, Liverpool

1943 BULLSHIT

I read in the *Express* that they've shot another German spy. His photograph looked pathetic. Why do they shoot spies? Why do they pretend they're so wicked, like murderers? At least *their* spies are wicked; I suppose *ours* are gallant men doing a wonderful job, giving their lives for their country ... and I suppose the Germans are telling their people the same thing. Why don't both sides agree to just put captured spies in a POW camp? Who'd be the loser? They couldn't do any more harm.

It's the same with the U-boats. They're cowardly murdering swine, the scum of the sea, because they attack unarmed merchant ships without warning. I heard a destroyer captain talking on the radio; he said when they'd sunk a U-boat, they collected bits of the dead German sailors in buckets out of the water, and everybody cheered. If U-boats are the 'jackals of the sea' what does that make the crews of our own submarines, who, it is announced, have just sunk another German merchant ship off Norway? If that destroyer captain was introduced to a

British submarine captain, would he call him a murdering scum too?

My Cousin Gordon calls this kind of talk bullshit. He says 'Bullshit baffles brains.'

Boy, aged thirteen, Tyneside

CHAPTER 13

THE HOME FRONT

Princess Elizabeth broadcasting to the children of the nation 'with my sister, Margaret Rose', at the height of the peril, October 1940. By 1945, Princess Elizabeth was Junior Officer in the ATS, learning to service heavy lorries.

THE OILY WIZARD

I was often bombed in the war, but never afraid. Tense, when a screaming-bomb was coming down, and I was counting to ten to see if I was going to go on living or not. But only *afraid* once; when my mate caught diphtheria and I thought he'd given it to me.

I wasn't afraid because of my father, who I regarded as some kind of wizard. A very oily wizard; the foreman–fitter at the gasworks. Even before the war, I regarded him as a wizard; sometimes he'd forget his 'bait' and Mam would send me down with his bait-tin, wrapped in a red spotted handkerchief. I would creep into the great smoking, steaming gasworks, beneath the window of the time-office man (who for some reason I always regarded as a mortal enemy), then I would wander about till a 'real' workman, with blackened face, asked me what I wanted. Then a group would gather.

'It's Bobbie's lad. Go an' fetch Bobbie. Where's he working?'

In an instant my father would emerge, black as the rest with shining white teeth, so I could hardly recognize him. Always two or three men walking with him, asking what to do. He was always in a hurry; not flustered, but driving on through an endless sea of problems like a black tramp-steamer. I always regarded the works as my father's kingdom, gorgeously evil-smelling, mysterious. There *was* a manager; but he only saw to the paper-work for my father ... My father loathed paper; he would defile it with his black thumbprints, then toss it aside with total contempt. His biggest condemnation was: 'It's all right on paper, but it'll never work in practice.'

My father's body was part of his wizardry. His thumbnail grew in five parallel segments, where he'd 'hit it with a hammer at the old North-eastern' as an apprentice. I used to press it, to see if it hurt him. It didn't. He would scrub himself when he came home, but could never quite get rid of the black grease, so that he had the shadowed eyes and swarthy good-looks of the silent-film star, Rudolph Valentino. He always polished his shoes, but never his work boots, which lay by the gas stove, black, caked and dreadful. His work overcoat reeked of benzene, ammonia and gas. He never had colds; because, he said, the germs couldn't live in the gasworks air. The primary school beneath the high gasworks wall didn't have colds, either. And somehow his heavy smoking was part of the strong-smelling mystery; the split thumbnail was an awesome brown; when he cut me a piece of bread, it would taste faintly of nicotine. He smoked in the outside toilet (my mother was terrified that for some reason this would lead to him setting himself on fire) and there too, during air raids, the lingering smell of him was a comfort.

He did miraculous things; one day he brought home a full-sized model of a Vickers machine-gun he'd made for me at work. Another time a three-foot model of HMS *Exeter*, victor of the River Plate. He could mend *anything*. Cabinets and model galleons flowed from his non-stop fingers. The cupboards were full of broken brass lumps of model machinery he'd made as an apprentice. And there were his five huge green books, full of drawings of reciprocating triple-expansion engines that I stared at for hours in awed incomprehension.

When war broke out, he became a section-leader in the wardens; it was just an extension of his wizardry. As foreman, he wore a filthy boilersuit; as a warden, a clean one. Wardens clustered round him as he walked, just like the workmen. He knew more about the raids than anybody else. He'd come home from work and say 'There's still a yellow alert on. The buggers is hanging around somewhere.' (Red alert meant the siren had gone.) He knew where raids had taken place; where they'd been bad; where an enemy bomber had been shot down. He always gave the impression of being in good control of the situation. He never used dramatic words like 'Hun' or 'Nazi'; always 'them buggers' said in the same tone of voice he might use about a stroppy Irish boilermaker, or the Nigerian labourer who always went for a snooze in the heat of the retort-house.

They came for him at any hour of the day or night. When he was home, my mother dreaded the knock on the door, the anxious black-capped figure with the inevitable question 'Is Bobbie in?' Sometimes, when he had dropped to sleep in a chair, exhausted, she used to tell them he'd gone out. But he always

Wardens in their post, in company with a special constable. Only a garden hut, but the nerve centre of a whole suburb. Note the shelf for lost-and-found gasmasks.

slept with one ear cocked; she was always pulled up in the middle of her lies by his call of 'Who's there, Maggie?'

During raids, he toured his district, talking to the people in the shelters. He always believed in telling people what was going on. Anything was better than the chaotic series of thuds, bangs, crumps, whistlings and hisses that was an air raid. Women used to stop my mother in the street and thank her for my father 'keeping an eye on them'.

He seemed to go through air raids with the wonder and gusto of a small boy. He would talk of the weird beauty of the 'Chandeliers' – the marvellous cages of blue lights that dropped slowly by parachute, lighting the target for the German bombers; he liked it even better when the ack-ack gunners blew them to bits. One night he heard the soft whispering of a cluster of incendiaries coming down, straight above his head. Just managed to get under a costermonger's barrow before they hit. Then there was a ring of them burning around him, and several burning through the barrow on top of him, and he thought 'his last moment had come'. He escaped by taking a flying kick at one of them, to make a gap to run through.

'Scored a goal, an' all!'

All night through we listened for his footsteps; the clink of hobnailed warden's boots. Mostly they'd walk steadily, even when German bombers were overhead. But sometimes they'd start to run, and then we'd hear the whistle of the bombs. He'd come through the shelter door-curtain in a flying leap, and land on his knees between the bunks with a shelter-shaking thud. Then sit up and say, 'By, I could do wi' a drop o' coffee, hinny.'

My mother only worried when he was on night shift at the gasworks. Climbing the ladders of the great gasholder, to kick burning incendiaries off the thin top plates. Chipping ice off a conveyor a hundred feet up, with a raid in progress. All he would say is 'I'm all right. I know those old works better than bleddy Hitler.'

He seemed to love it all. In 1939, he had incipient stomach ulcers; they seemed to vanish on 3 September. He always said it was the meat-shortage cured his stomach; I think it was the danger. My dearest ambition was to reach the age of fifteen, and be his official ARP messenger. Sadly, the end of the war beat me to it.

Boy, Tyneside

MY MOTHER'S WAR

My mother was always very calm; I only saw her go to pieces once. To listen to her, the only important thing about the war was getting enough cigarettes for my father. Father never sat still between 1939 and 1945. All that kept him going was twenty full-strength Capstan a day. Without nicotine, he was like a Spitfire without petrol. Some of his mates would call at the shop on their way to work. If the shop had fags, they'd go on to work; if not, they'd go back to bed.

So crisis-point for Mam was Friday afternoons, when she walked round the whole town, looking for cigarettes. She was pretty, in a ladylike way, and had a lot of charm, all of which was used on the tobacconists. It used to outrage me; we'd be walking round the town in the rain, and she'd be giving me stick cos she was fed-up, then at the tobacconist's door she'd turn on the charm like a searchlight. I once called her a hypocrite, and nearly got a clout.

Worst were the shops that only had Turkish cigarettes – you'd see a horrible little hand-lettered sign in the shop window – PASHAS ONLY. My father said Pashas were made from camel dung. But they were better than nothing. Only, if she was offered them early-on, she didn't know what to do. If she bought Pashas, she wouldn't be able to afford better cigarettes further on round the town . . .

When we got to Gran's for tea, Dad would have got there from work. He'd be smoking half-inch dog-ends, burning his nose with the match as he lit them. Or just sitting there panting. Mam would always play a trick on him – get any Pashas out of her shopping-bag first and watch his face fall. Then she'd bury the Pashas with Gold Flake and Players, and every packet she pulled out, his face would light up more. And her face used to look

Housewives finished their shopping lists with 'AUC' – 'Anything Under Counter'. Cigarettes were one shilling for twenty.

so proud, like she'd presented him with a bouncing baby boy.

In 1941, any woman's most prized possession was a pair of 'Russian' fur-lined boots. Unobtainable in the shops, with or without clothing coupons. But Dad met a 'chap at work' who had two pairs for sale, Mam's size. Mam asked what colour they were – Dad hadn't bothered to ask. Mam had a very subtle taste in colour – Dad's taste could only be described as 'garish'.

That night, he brought home a superb pair of boots, which were quite the foulest shade of acid-green I have ever seen before or since. Mam stared at them in agony.

'I thought they looked bonny,' said Dad.

Silence.

'They'll mucky-down, given time . . .'

Silence.

'Well, they'll keep your feet warm, anyway . . .'

Silence.

'I'd have got the other pair, only they were only a dull brown . . .'

Mam weighed the boots in her hand, and contemplated Dad's head. Then 'They're lovely', she said, with a smile of pure agony.

I wakened one winter night in 1942, with a sense of something terribly wrong. The light was on in the sitting-room, and I could hear Mam wailing.

'Eeh, Bob, I wish you would come, I wish you would come.' (Dad was on night shift.) I could also hear the spaniel-dog howling. Hitler had got us at last.

I ran out in pyjamas. Mam was standing in the middle of the kitchen, wearing a raincoat over her nightdress, and holding an umbrella over her head. The kitchen was full of sparkling, falling rain, glinting in the lamplight. The dog was standing faithfully beside her, soaking wet and shaking himself every two minutes. The kitchen floor was an inch under water.

I could think of nothing to do but stand beside her. She turned to me and said 'Put your coat on, you'll catch your death.' And there we stood, paralysed, looking at the burst water-pipe like sun-worshippers stare at the sun; until our upstairs neighbour, old Jack Dawson, suddenly appeared in response to my mother's wails, seized a huge hammer and beat the water-pipe flat with three blows of terrible violence.

The sparkling rain stopped. My mother came out of her paralysis.

'Thank you, Jack. Could you do with a cup of tea?' And she began, like a mended toy, to sweep the water out of the kitchen with a broom.

And that was the only time I saw her beaten, in the whole war.

Boy, Tyneside

1941 SALVAGE

On one occasion, following a government scrap-metal collection (aluminium teapots, pans etc.) a story spread around amongst the children that if you collected a bag of shrapnel and took it to the local army barracks, you would receive a toy. Using a spare kitbag of my father's I spent many weeks gathering shrapnel from people's gardens and backyards. When I finally gathered what I thought was a lot (about 30 lb.) I took it to the barracks which was about three miles away. Upon arriving, I was thrilled to see many boxes, sacks and bags of shrapnel outside the gates. Two soldiers with rifles and fixed bayonets were marching up and down on guard duty. I approached them, dragging my bag and asked them where did I go for the toy? One soldier began to swear at me and the other turned round and pointed his rifle and bayonet at me, shouting he would 'stick it in my behind if I did not clear off'. I ran a short distance, leaving the bag, and tried to impress the soldiers by telling them my father was in their regiment (which he was) but they were not impressed and still chased me.

Boy, Liverpool

Aluminium to make Spitfires – anything from silver paper to colanders and circular hot-water bottles. This 'plane' is being built in Sidcup, Kent.

FROM WASTE PAPER TO MUNITIONS OF WAR

1941 METAL

Metal was in short supply. Park railings were cut down with acetylene torches, and taken away to be melted down. Yet there were some first-rate metal toys to be had – Spitfires, Hurricanes, Wellingtons, and ships of the Royal Navy. I was particularly proud of my little fleet, which consisted of the battleships HMS *Hood* and *Nelson*, the cruiser *Exeter* and two or three nameless submarines which stood less than a centimetre high at the conning tower. I had some grand naval battles on the lounge carpet, with my submarines carefully submerged under the long Indian pile, a trap for any unwary person who crossed the room in stockinged feet. When we heard the news that the *Hood* was sunk, I could hardly believe it. How could anything defeat a ship with such a formidable array of guns? After that, I could take no more pleasure in my games.

I still had the ships but their magic was gone, and although I still played with the others occasionally, it seemed kind of cheating to use my favourite ship.

Boy, aged twelve, Manchester

COMEDIANS

In some ways I remember the war as a series of wireless programmes. Not just the historic broadcasts of Chamberlain and Churchill, not the faultless King's English of Alvar Liddell and the other announcers, but also the comedians. Arthur Askey with his 'silly songs', Jack Warner with his blue catalogue of unlikely jobs (putting the seeds in raspberry jam). I liked Rob Wilton as the hesitant Mr Muddlecombe.

'The day war broke out ... my missus said to me ... "What are you going to *do* about it?"'

'I said "What ... me?"'

'She said "Well ... you and a few thousand others."'

But the universal favourite was Tommy Handley, the irrepressible Mayor of Foaming-at-the-Mouth. The secret of his charm was in his voice – rich, warm, friendly, chirpy ... everyone's favourite naughty uncle. Most of the humour depended on catch-phrases which we all knew and used, reassuringly, in our own lives. If we had a present to give and felt embarrassed about it, we could borrow the words of the ITMA char, Mrs Mopp.

'I've brought this for you, sir. It's one of the lodger's leavings.'

If we felt neglected, our protest was ready-made for us.

'Don't forget the diver, sir, don't forget the diver.'

Every newspaper left neatly bundled by the dustbin was regarded as a direct poke in the eye for Hitler. This lady in her 'turban' was the height of chic, and was trying to make bombcases seductive. The 'turban' became popular in the factories, where it stopped most women with long hair from being scalped or killed by having their hair caught in moving machinery.

One catch-phrase in particular neatly sums up my experience of 1939 to 1945. 'Don't you know there's a war on?'

On the whole, I don't believe I did.

Boy, aged fifteen, Manchester

AWFUL WARNING

My mother often said to me 'The Germans will come for you if you are a naughty girl.'

This led to vivid pictures in my mind of a German soldier climbing through my bedroom window, to literally take me from my bed whilst I was asleep. I went to bed night after night, almost afraid to go to sleep, wondering if the Germans would come for me during that night. (I do not remember being particularly naughty either.)

If we went for a Sunday afternoon walk I would close *all* the windows prior to going, to prevent the Germans getting in.

This gave me an extreme fear of the dark, because I feared being taken away by night. This fear of the dark has dominated me for years.

Girl, aged five, Warwickshire

Was there a boy with soul so dead he didn't want to be a fighter pilot, even if, like me, he was short-sighted and too fat to get into a cockpit?

Amateurs and proud of it – rebels without hats or tunics, and most with their hands in their pockets ... the total opposite of the regimented goose-stepping hordes. Only the dog-mascot and Brylcreem were compulsory. The fighter is a Hawker Typhoon, which makes the year 1944, but the pattern was set in 1940, their casualness as compulsive as German rigidity.

The 'little war helper' theme at its worst. Who do you blame – the kids who posed, the newspaper that printed it, the Ministry of Information who encouraged it, or the public who cooed over it? A photograph from Worthing, Sussex, January 1941.

1942 THE GERMANS HAVE COME TO GET ME!

With there being a lot in our family we had to share rooms, and in the summer especially it got very hot and so we used to open the window. Because the room was very dark it didn't matter about the blackout.

The bunk-beds lay with their foot against the window. I had to go on the top bunk but I didn't mind. One night during the summer it was very hot and stuffy and our Mam came in and opened the window. We all fell asleep with the wind blowing in. The curtains gently rose and fell again.

All of a sudden there was a loud scream from our bedroom. My Mam and Dad rushed in to see what was up. The curtain had caught around my foot and then the wind had tugged it. I thought it was the Germans trying to pull me out through the window.

Boy, aged three, Liverpool

The war felt like this 90 per cent of the time — no fire in the grate, not enough light to read by properly, blackout outside, and the newspaper headlines clung to and fed off as if they were a blood transfusion. A picture without deceit or propaganda.

MINISTRY OF HEALTH SAYS—

COUGHS AND SNEEZES SPREAD DISEASES—

trap the germs in your handkerchief

HELP TO KEEP THE NATION FIGHTING FIT

Another piece of misplaced Government zeal — handkerchiefs, constantly flapped about, spread more germs than sneezing. Still — the words stuck. They were a 'pre-TV jingle', quoted at you by friends every time you sneezed until the 1950s.

Perhaps the finest victory of Home Front propaganda – the diminishing of the greatest evil the twentieth century has known into a pair of incompetent clowns. Churchill had a fair hand in the denigration process. Mussolini was 'the puffed-up bullfrog from the Pontine Marshes'. Hitler's true name was discovered to be the ridiculous 'Schickelgruber'. He was the little corporal, the failed housepainter who foamed at the mouth and chewed the grass when he was thwarted. I think we got through the perils of 1940 by snobbishly sharing Churchill's aristocratic contempt for a working-class German. We were convinced Hitler knew he was inferior. It is only recently that I have grasped the true strength of the Nazi war-machine, and what peril we really stood in. For once, total non-grasp of reality was a real strength.

The same theme again – Churchill's moral superiority over Hitler. By this time (April 1944) Hitler may really have been frightened – but he was frightened at the crushing superiority of material in the American and Russian war-machines. At Yalta, Churchill was already a fading third to Stalin and Roosevelt.

KEM'S ' HITLER'S NIGHTMARE '

HAPPY YEARS

For me, the war years were happy. We had more freedom than we would have done had the men been at home. We were allowed to roam in the woodlands and on the golf course without supervision. Parents didn't fear lurking prowlers in lonely places, as they assumed all the men who might do us harm were busily occupied.

Girl, Sheffield. From Norman Longmate, How We Lived Then, *Hutchinson, 1971*

We loved the squander bug, because he made a fool out of grown-ups. The swastikas on him were only part of the joke – really he was a British, and purely malicious, child. We enjoyed his antics, and cheerfully spent every penny we could lay our hands on. He had as much effect on our finances as 'Desperate Dan' or 'Lord Snooty'.

A lamp-post gang in Britain's 'front-line town': Dover, March 1941. Before the war, gas lamp-posts were our favourite rendezvous on winter evenings, giving heat as well as light. We hid secret messages in their hollow bases, swung from their cast-iron arms by ropes and bike tyres. Here the lamp base has been painted with white rings, to make it visible in the blackout. Sandbags have been tied to it with string, for use against incendiary bombs. They were much patronized by dogs, and burst when lifted, showering evil-smelling sand. One boy is carrying a fence-paling as a spear. We all went armed, then.

1942 WE SHALL FIGHT THEM IN THE PARKS

Once the heavy raids were over, we were allowed more liberty, especially in the long summer evenings. We formed a gang in our road, and fought rival gangs who trespassed. Then I read *The Scarlet Pimpernel* by Baroness Orczy and that really got things going. We all had code-names and would not answer our real ones. We found the witches' code in a book, and practised writing it. I found a button in my mother's button-box, and pinched some red sealing-wax – this became the Scarlet Pimpernel seal, and I sealed all orders to the gang. We met in Queen's Park, halfway between school and our road. Messages were left in a hollow tree, high up. Then we got the idea of using bows and arrows in case the Germans invaded. We used to practise in the park, sharpening our arrows and lengthening our shots. Sometimes the park keeper chased us off, but we hid in the bushes and, when he had gone, went on practising. Then my brother was employed to ride his three-wheeler bike in a maniac way to distract old Parky from our war-preparations. He got walloped once, but we didn't retaliate on Parky – we thought that would draw unwelcome notice.

We practised every night and Saturday mornings. I once had

the disgraceful experience of being taken to be fitted with new shoes on a Saturday morning.

We clubbed together with our pocket-money and bought a first-aid kit – archery is hard on the hands. The boys got a large number of knives, but they were not allowed to bring them into our camp, which was in the bombed house opposite ours; the knives were strictly for use on the Germans only.

Because I could shoot the furthest, and was oldest, I was gang leader. Our only punishment for breaking the rules was being chucked out and not defended by the gang against other gangs – a really serious punishment.

Girl, aged eight, London

Monty, second only to Churchill, was the 'star' of our side. He was, of course, a card, wildly eccentric, like our comic-heroes 'Desperate Dan', the ever scruffy 'Wolf of Kabul', and the immortal ragged 'Wilson'. He wore two badges on his beret, and a jumper – unlike the pompous bemedalled 'Colonel Blimps' who had lost the early battles of the war.

1944 MONTY

At school we discussed the merits of British Generals like modern boys discuss footballers. Monty, like Churchill, had star quality. His beret was almost as well known as Churchill's cigar and V-sign. One day our enterprising headmaster announced that Monty was passing through the district, and had been prevailed on to talk to us. Our old man, we said proudly, could wangle anything.

And so real armoured-cars rolled up the unadopted road that led to the school, and Monty himself strode on to the stage in the hall and gave us five minutes' brisk advice on never being afraid to take responsibility.

Boy, aged fifteen, Manchester

1942–3 SMALL SCHOOL – BIG WAR

2 November 1942 The Headmaster arrived to find the Army ~~in~~ command. An A A gun was in position on the playing-field, five large tents with troops in occupation and a large hole in the fencing through which the gun had been dragged. The gun had arrived on Sat 31 October, the day when this area was attacked without warning. The nearness of the gun to the school caused some alarm and fear that it might attract counter-attack, so it was decided the children would go to the shelter at the first hint and not wait for the red alert. A stream of visitors, civilian and military, came to study the situation, to determine the amount of damage done to the fencing, and the disturbance caused by the presence of the gun and soldiers.

January 1943 Ink in inkwells frozen this morning. More burst pipes to contend with. No records of life on the school field, but one can make a guess and shudder.

October 1943 It is reported the troops are connecting their hut to the water supply here. That hole in the fence is still causing trouble, because through it came cattle to eat the crops in the school vegetable gardens, and on 29 October Mr Prior had to complain about the damage to lawns, paths and playground caused by the army lorries. More visitors came to inspect, but who paid, and to whom they paid, if they paid, is not recorded.

The wooden hut became ex-army in 1944, and was badly damaged in 1945. The Headmaster does not know who is responsible for it. (The hut ended its days in 1961, when it was sold to become a henhouse.)

GASMASKS – AFTER ALL THIS TIME!

29 November 1943 The County Police Mobile Gas Van visited to test those gasmasks so long carried and still ready. All except two worked perfectly. One was too big and obviously not the one issued. One had a hole in it which fortunately was discovered before the child went into the van.

MAY 1942 A CHANGE OF HEART

I'm sitting in the warm sunshine writing this. The weather is so gorgeous that it's a great temptation to spend much of the time punting on the river, instead of working.

Yesterday I marched in a May Day procession, to demonstrate Anglo-Soviet Unity, through the streets and parks. The Home

We ran alongside parades, to make them last longer. After 1942, life grew so boring that even two dogs fighting was an event. Looking back, it all seems so amateur.

Guard band marched in front, but were sometimes not sure of what they were supposed to be playing, which caused some amusement. They finally broke into a very slow and sentimental rendering of the 'Volga Boat Song' which proved most difficult to march to.

In the Easter vacation I went to Birmingham to a student congress. I hitch-hiked with another girl, there and back. We travelled mostly on lorries which is much pleasanter than going by train or car, as lorry-drivers are very interesting to talk to; they told us about their families, about the loads they were carrying and the journeys they made every day and about the country we passed through. We felt we had learnt a lot about lorries and lorry-drivers by the time we got home.

Girl, aged nineteen, Cambridge

THE DEFENCE OF WITHERNSEA

We heard at school that a German bomber had been brought down south of Holmpton, after being spotted by searchlights at Skeffling. Following our usual practice, we rode our bicycles five miles to the crash. We approached by walking over the fields and were some little distance away when a large explosion occurred, shrapnel flew over our heads and a large cloud of smoke appeared. We turned tail. (Unknown to us, the aircraft carried two landmines and one had exploded, killing some of the bomb-disposal team.)

Next day we went again, to find that the guards, fearful of a second explosion, had withdrawn to the farmhouse and left the wreck unguarded. The tail had broken off and was some 150 yards away, while the main body of the aircraft lay partly in and over a ditch. The aircraft had not burned.

The farmhouse containing the guards was out of sight over the hill, so myself and at least fifteen other kids had free access. I remember I stood on a large cylinder painted dark grey-green (that turned out later to have been the remaining landmine). Various people took objects they fancied as souvenirs. Alec Allen took the radio set, Ian Wilkinson the top of the control-column, Tony Cockerill a pair of flying-gloves and myself the altimeter.

Then we found the guns: a machine-gun with ammo in upright containers, and an aircraft-cannon with belt-ammunition. We carried the cannon and machine-gun, plus three hundred rounds for the machine-gun and about 200 rounds in belt for the cannon, and laid them under bushes well away from the crash. We returned home and went back after dark to collect our guns, transporting our loot home on Tony Cockerill's mother's bicycle.

Not all of us were in the choir, but as I had a tower-key and in those days the church was never locked, we hid the guns in the 'pulley room' of the church tower. It was a three-foot space, above the ringer's chamber and below the belfry, running the whole width of the tower and without windows.

As most of us were in the Air Training Corps, we reckoned we knew about guns, and we did know enough to strip and clean both weapons. We also knew the dangers of firing a round up a crash-distorted barrel, so after cleaning the guns, we smuggled them out of the church and on to the beach. We put a round in each, laid the guns on a sack, and tied long strings to the triggers. We then retreated behind an outcrop of cliff, and pulled on the strings. The first was the machine-gun, and all went well. But the cannon not only jumped off the sack, but sent a large ball of fire out to sea ... We did not know the colour-codings for German ammunition and had chosen a tracer-round for the cannon.

As thumps and bangs were commonplace in those days we had no fear of being caught from the noise, and we smuggled the guns back to the tower.

In those days the German bombers were in the habit of flying in very low over the coast, and often passed between St Nicholas Church and the 120-foot Withernsea lighthouse. Our idea was to set up the machine-gun on the north-east corner of the tower roof, and the cannon on the north-west corner. The weapons were to be tied down to the parapet with old bell-ropes, and we intended to shoot at the next aircraft, first with the machine-gun

Lovely loot. Left unguarded, they would be stripped bare by souvenir-hunting boys in a matter of hours. They still make my mouth water, like ripe peaches. Both pictures were taken in 1940, one in East Anglia, the other in Hampshire.

and follow with the cannon. That way we intended the aircraft to crash in the fields beyond the town and thus not do any damage. We had the ring-sight for the machine-gun and intended to 'follow tracer' with the cannon.

For the next two weeks there was not one raid, even though there was a full-moon period.

By this time, of course, the RAF had discovered the loss of various parts of the aircraft. No wonder, since Cecil Bickley had taken a hacksaw and sawn the swastika out of the tail. The RAF were hunting the guns, aided by the local police. The local inspector of special constabulary, Inspector Stathers, was surprised to find a perfect specimen of a German bomb-sight in his son Harold's wardrobe. Questions followed . . .

Several hasty conferences were held, near the lighthouse, by the choir and others who had stolen gear, as to how to dispose of it before being caught in possession. There were many lads up early next morning to dispose of gear in the dike bottoms (irrigation ditches).

Before long, the whole story was out. The guns and ammunition were collected from the church and taken to the local juvenile court in Railway Crescent on a builder's handcart. Sixteen of us were hauled before the court. There was a large table piled high with our loot.

The RAF sent down a young officer to prosecute. The vicar, the Rev. Willie Passmore, appeared to speak on our behalf. Some parents attended, including a certain Mr Todd, something of a political speaker locally and a strong supporter of the Workers' Education Association. He spoke with passion in defence of all the boys, and particularly his son Alfred, a pal of mine who confided in me afterwards his embarrassment, and said he wished his old man had shut up and paid the fine like everybody else.

At the time I thought the police and magistrates took a serious view of our escapade. But later, my father told me all the adults concerned were amused and sympathetic, and somewhat annoyed by the attitude of the RAF. It appeared the RAF were covering up a blunder and trying to save face. Later I realized our escapade must have resulted in some poor RAF person facing a charge.

We were all given a conditional discharge, and made to pay four shillings costs. There was severe criticism of the authorities for their failure to mount guards on the plane. The vicar wrote to the Archbishop of York, apologizing on behalf of his choirboys. The Archbishop's reply consisted of one line, and indicated his sympathies were with us boys.

The machine-gun had turned out to be an MG 41, of the latest type, and the RAF hadn't had a chance to inspect one before.

Boys, aged fourteen to fifteen, Withernsea, Humberside

1942–5 WEAPONS

I was sent away to a boarding-school, run by Dominican monks at Blackfriars in the Northampton countryside. I became interested in chemistry for its potential in making explosives, stink-bombs and smokescreens.

Not far away was a Polish camp. The Poles were reputed to fly their aircraft into the German planes when they ran out of ammunition, but security was not their strong point. After discreet investigation I chose a rainy day so I could ride through the park in my bicycle cape. The Poles were nowhere to be seen, and I opened the unlocked door of their armoury. Inside, I swathed myself with bandoliers of ammunition, resumed my cape and rode off. Back at the school, I emptied each cartridge into an Ovaltine tin, and built up my store of cordite.

It seemed to me that I would get a bigger haul if I paid a visit at night so that I could load a pack. So I broke out of school at midnight and crawled across a field. There was no need for this precaution, there were no sentries. As I entered the armoury I felt something under my feet; when I shone my torch I discovered I was standing on detonators which were scattered loose about the floor. This time I loaded up with Mills grenades and 2″ mortar bombs, and the following day in the boot-room I had an interesting time finding out how the safety mechanism of the mortar bomb worked with the help of a tin-opener.

I repaired to a gravel pit and threw the bomb over the edge. Unfortunately nothing happened, so I had to scramble down the side of the pit, stones bouncing around the bomb, in order to retrieve it and have another go. Finally I was obliged to lay a Mills grenade beside it; I withdrew the steel pin and inserted some sticks of cordite in its place, laying a fuse with further sticks of cordite which I ignited. This did the trick and produced a satisfying explosion.

One day a Flying Fortress crashed in the woods and we hared off to see what we could find. Several of us tried to haul a machine-gun out of it, but without success. However, one boy of unusual strength got it out on his own and was subsequently seen in the showers banging the butt on the floor, trying to fire the bullet that was in the breech.

Another boy recovered part of the jawbone of one of the air-crew, complete with teeth. This he passed round the refectory, which had the desired effect of putting a number of people off their meal, so that there was more for the others to eat.

Somehow or other our headmaster, the Bede, got to know that the school basement (where the boys' trunks were kept) was beginning to resemble the Houses of Parliament in the time of Guy Fawkes. He made an announcement; there would be an amnesty provided all was surrendered. I was in a dilemma. It was a sad thought to give up all of my trophies, but unfortunately my reputation was such that the Bede would never believe that I had nothing. He had been a bombardier in the First World War and I already had experience of the strength of his grenade-throwing arm.

I appeared at the eleventh hour and he greeted me with a beam; he knew he could rely on me. The police were exceedingly impressed with the size of the collection, which included machine-guns, and several anti-tank rocket-launchers, complete with missiles.

Back home in the holidays, Mike and I broke into an unexploded bomb dump and recovered a Blacker Bombard, which we strapped to the carrier of his bicycle and rode home in daylight without a soul saying a word. Perhaps everyone was getting punch-drunk towards the end of the war. My father discovered it and said it would have to go. He simply telephoned the police. 'I have a bomb. Would you please come and collect it.'

In order to liven things up we started making our own bombs with calcium chlorate and sulphur. This mixture was stuffed into a metal tube and sealed with a plug containing a piece of high-resistance wire. Twin wires were run out to a safe distance and connected to a grid-bias battery. Every Saturday, the quarry behind the Isolation Hospital resounded to the crashes of our endeavours. On the way home people would be standing in the road trying to make out where the bombs had been dropped from. We each had our own detonation-boxes, complete with battery, reel of wire, and switch; the lid covered with linoleum worked with a tasteful pattern.

My last acquisition was a 9 mm automatic pistol, but I had trouble getting satisfactory ammunition for it and sold it to somebody for a fiver.

I have always been grateful I wasn't a parent in those days. When my wife read this she said didn't I realize I was stealing?

I had to admit we thought of it as the spoils of war.

Boy, aged twelve to fifteen, Northants

CHAPTER 14 THE AMERICAN INVASION

1941 AMERICA I LOVE YOU

'Japanese planes have attacked Pearl Harbor.' I spent the whole weekend in a daze. *Ridiculous* that America and Japan should fight! I'd read an American comic only a month before, in which American fighters were defending San Francisco against Japanese bombers (they all had open cockpits and fixed wheels with *spats – jokes* by comparison with Spitfires); and I thought: how silly – how can they fight when they're on opposite sides of the world? Science fiction, like the Martians fighting the Venusians . . .

Then Hitler declared war on America, and I *knew* he was mad. Yes, I spent the whole weekend wandering in a daze, and one American song kept running through my brain.

> America I love you, you're like a mother to me . . .
> From ocean to ocean, this sudden emotion . . .

And America became magic. The things we heard of! Bulldozers that could build a whole airfield in twenty-four hours. Liberty ships built in a week, from the first plate being laid. The Americans were going to build 25,000 planes a year . . . there had only been 3,000 on *both* sides in the Battle of Britain. The war had become, as we soon learnt to say, 'a different ball-game'.

American comics flooded in; new heroes like Superman and Dick Tracy, the cop with the two-way wrist-TV and nose like a rectangular kite. And jazz records we learnt to listen to the American way, heads neck-breakingly on one side, nodding wisely in time with the music, clicking our fingers to the rhythm and, if possible, chewing gum. They seemed all about travel, those records. We were urged to 'Take the "A" Train' or the 'Chattanooga Choochoo', especially on 'Route 66'. Americans were always arriving or departing.

We learnt that Betty Grable had the best legs in the world, and had them insured for a million dollars (the word 'million' was on every lip). Better still, she was married to Harry James, who could play 'The Flight of the Bumble Bee' on the trumpet, faster than it had ever been played before.

There came a dreadful rumour (the first one not concerned with the war for two years) that she had died in childbirth.

Our other hero was Fats Waller, the huge negro who invented Boogie Woogie. Every kid who was allowed near a piano could play the left-hand roll of Boogie Woogie. Fats talked to himself as he played, a shocking thing till you got used to it. We had just got used to it when he died of pneumonia. It seemed a very serious blow to the War Effort.

There were two gods of the clarinet, Benny Goodman and Artie Shaw. (I refused to believe that the American 'Artie' was only a shortening of the mundane English name 'Arthur' – I had a fight with another kid over that.) Both had their supporters, who argued interminably about their virtues, as if they were Arsenal and Tottenham Hotspur. For a while, we quite forgot the War.

But even there, the Yanks were tops. We abandoned our faithful Hurricanes and Spitfires, which had only won the Battle of Britain. The American fighters had much more exciting names, even *swearing* names, like the Grumman Hellcat. Above all, there was the Flying Fortress, that carried so many guns and flew in such tight groups six miles high, that no German fighter would dare come near it. And it had a bomb-sight so accurate that it could drop a bomb into a pickle-barrel from 20,000 feet ...

And the American troop carriers, huge four-engined monoplanes called 'Stratocruiser' and 'Constellation' that made our old biplanes look like rubbish from the Science Museum.

I made an impassioned speech in our school debating-society, about the superiority of all things American. My beloved English teacher kept tripping me up, stopping me for saying things like 'Th'Americans' instead of 'The Americans'. I couldn't understand it, he'd always been sympathetic to me before ...

Of course, the gilt eventually got knocked off the gingerbread. The Hellcat, for all its name, didn't do too well against the Japanese Zero. And the Americans kept on shortening their line, and making strategic withdrawals, just like we'd been doing ever since 1940 ... Then some Americans got stationed at Whitley Bay, and people started saying there were three things wrong with them: they were 'overpaid, oversexed and over here'. They had a fight with the Australian Air Force on the sea-front, and the Australians threw several of them through the plate-glass windows of shops.

Boy, aged thirteen, Tyneside

This is how they will always be to us: jeep-driving, gum-chewing, physically arrogant, infinitely more glamorous even than the RAF's 'Brylcreem Boys'. Overpaid, oversexed and over here. Adults and males loathed them. The kids and girls loved them.

BOYFRIENDS

My father was posted to India with the RAF. In early 1940, the Army took away the family's two cars. While my Dad was away my Mum had lots of American and Polish boyfriends. In this way we got a little more food. I used to grease my pedal-car with butter.

Boy, aged nine, Liverpool

AN AMERICAN BOYFRIEND

When I first got interested in men, I brought an American boy-friend home. I really liked this man, and I think he liked me. At the same time, my cousin (who was only a baby) was living with us. He picked the same day as I brought my boyfriend home to 'poo' all over the hall. When my boyfriend came in he slipped on it, went head over heels and landed on his face in it. I've never seen him since.

Girl, aged sixteen, Liverpool

BOXES OF SWEETS

There was an American air-base near where I lived and my aunty was courting an American called Mike. One night a German plane was shot down at Hooton Airfield and the pilot escaped and was on the run. A car drove down the road with a loudspeaker; a man was telling everyone to lock their doors and stay inside.

My mother decided we should all go down the shelter! But as we were leaving the house there came a knock at the front door. She opened the door a little bit and saw a man panting. He had his head halfway through the doorway when my mother tried to shut the door. He had his head trapped in the door and he was trying to say who he was. He finally made himself understood. He was Mike. The next day we heard the German had been caught. When Mike used to visit my aunty he used to bring boxes of sweets for me and Pat.

Girl, aged fourteen, Liverpool

1942–3   AN AMERICAN GIFT

I remember the kindness and generosity of the American GIs, our horror at the Free French sailors who would crack open and eat raw mussels on the beach at Barmouth, and a visit I made to the Polish army camp on the other side of the estuary. Just before Christmas I was collecting holly in the Arthog area. I missed a train to Barmouth, and after trudging through woods and swamps, knocked on the door of the Polish army camp near the far end of Barmouth viaduct.

The Polish troops must have thought I looked a cold, wet, pathetic sight, and handed me a pint mug of tea and a doorstep of bread and cheese, which seemed to be the only food they were having for their tea. Cold and wet that I was, I remember feeling sorry for the spartan rations that the Poles seemed to have and could hardly finish eating the thick chunk of bread.

There were servicemen of many nations in Barmouth, and we besieged them with requests for foreign stamps and coins.

By some means my London evacuee pal, Peter Adamson, or myself had come by the princely sum of sixpence and were debating how to best expend this when my youngest brother came on the scene. I'm afraid that we could not include him in our plans with only sixpence. He followed us down the road to Barmouth, bawling his head off.

A lone American soldier who was strolling along, called him over and presented him with half-a-crown. I'm afraid we immediately descended on my brother and had a three-way split – chips at 2*d.* a bag, fish at 6*d.* and lemonade 5*d.* from the local chip shop.

Boy, aged nine, Barmouth

CHAPTER 15 PRISONERS OF WAR

1940 RELUCTANT HEROES

We went for a couple of days' holiday in a village near Bethesda in North Wales.

A German bomber came over our heads and crashed into the mountainside. The crew got out, and in good English they explained how they had just eaten in a Paris restaurant which was very nice.

They said that the war was tragic and useless and would result in decadence, if we did not accept a 'Plan' for Europe.

Both seemed to become prisoners quite gladly, once the soldiers arrived, saying it was all over, no one would care for you, if you died fighting or not.

Girl, aged seventeen, Liverpool

1940 GERMAN CHOCOLATE

We only had one big raid on Chester, in daylight. A German pilot came down by parachute. My father, who was a special constable, went to arrest him. A big crowd had gathered and were just watching him, not knowing what to do. I think the pilot was quite glad to be arrested; he gave my father some chocolate. My father gave it to me. It was in a little round tin box. I didn't eat it, because the Germans were rumoured to poison that kind of thing. We've still got it . . . I think it was part of his survival ration.

How the Government wanted the public to imagine them – obedient and well guarded.

Boy, aged seven, Chester

1942–3 TRAINLOADS OF POWs

As the tides of war swayed in our favour, trainloads of German POWs arrived at Northwich Station, often as the evening was drawing to a close. They were lined up four abreast and marched down Station Road and along the cinder track that led across the Flashes to Marbury Hall. I and hundreds of other youths often went to watch their arrival, to hoot, jeer and shout at these our enemies, whole lines of unkempt men, with few possessions, unshaven, weary, red-eyed and in some cases ill-clad, these once-proud remnants of Hitler's armies, escorted by perhaps a dozen or so armed troops, as they marched the two or three miles to their camp.

Gradually people became used to these arrivals, and feelings towards them gradually tempered. The Italian POWs were the first allowed out of camp to work on farms and in local factories, including ICI.

My Dad was in the lorry business. We had two Germans to help him. They had to eat outside in the barn. My mother was always soft-hearted; she came in one day and said, 'Have you seen what they've given those poor lads for their dinners? A scrap of dry bread and a scrap of sausage. You can't expect a man to do a day's work on that!' Soon she was giving them their dinner. In the end, we had them in for Sunday dinner. One of them had been the only tiger-tamer in Europe before the war – he said there were plenty of lion-tamers but only one tiger-tamer. He pulled open his shirt and showed me where a tiger had mauled him – a terrible scar from his neck all the way down to his belt. Captain Something, he called himself, when he was a tiger-tamer. We became great friends. We still send Christmas cards at Christmas.

Boy, aged thirteen, Cheshire

1943–5 CAMP ORCHESTRA

Some hundreds of prisoners, not considered a high security risk, came to Marbury Hall.

I remember practising the piano one afternoon, and seeing a German POW, who was engaged in hedge-cutting for the local farmer, spending a long time on the piece immediately in front of our house. When we got into conversation with him it turned out he had been a cathedral organist in Germany and he was delighted to listen to anyone playing Bach, even a beginner like me.

He always lingered after that, when we played classical 78 records, with the window open.

A music teacher in Hartford and her husband invited home a German musician, August Wusterbecker, captured at Ostend. By this time, Wusterbecker, who was not only a violinist but also a conductor, had formed a camp orchestra. Instruments were loaned by local musicians. Paul Voigt, a violin-maker and restorer, supplied a cello and one or two double-basses were actually made in the camp. The problem of dress was overcome by blackout material being used to make a rough type of evening-dress. My family were invited to concerts and it was a great treat for me, because travel to Manchester to hear the Hallé wasn't possible due to petrol-rationing.

August Wusterbecker remained in the camp till 1949, and I was privileged to receive some violin-lessons from him. He knew little English, but we managed.

The Rotary Club arranged for local people in certain professions to invite home for Sunday lunch prisoners who had been of the same profession in Germany. My father asked home two German bankers, as he was the manager of our local building society.

Boy, aged fourteen, Cheshire

1944 WOPS AND JERRIES

When I went to help my friends in Cumberland with their harvest in 1944, I was outraged to see POWs helping as well. No security; an army lorry with canvas top pulled up at the farm gate, the driver banged on his door and shouted 'Out, you idle Wops' and three woebegone figures in brown leapt down from the tailgate and stood clutching bundles and shivering in the morning air.

They were known as 'Alfonso', 'Luigi' and 'That Useless Bugger' none of which were their real names. To the farmers, the first one you got was Alfonso and the second Luigi. Not knowing a word of English, they had learnt to answer to these names, like pet dogs. It helped *us* distinguish them. 'You Useless Bugger' answered his name as cheerfully as the rest.

Alfonso and Luigi were very small – five foot four. Swarthy, hook-nosed, big-brown-eyed, they might have been twins, though they were not related. They did everything together – never more than four feet apart. The farmer had learnt not to separate them – they got miserable and their work went off. Even in the heat of midday, they kept on their greatcoats and rolled-up balaclava helmets.

The farmer said they were good little workers, because they came from the North – car-workers in Milan before the war. All the ones from the North were hard workers. Those from the South were totally idle; no farmer wanted them, but they had to accept one Southerner for every two Northerners. Rationing!

That Useless Bugger (always uttered with total contempt) was from the South. Bigger – about five foot seven, slender, with a trim black moustache and arrogant air. He'd stop work the moment the farmer's eye was off him; drift away to where the two land-girls were working like, as the farmer said 'a tom-cat on heat'. Very handsome, like Douglas Fairbanks, with a flashy smile and perfect white teeth. But as far as the land-girls were concerned, he didn't exist. He had learnt one English phrase – 'I can see the top of your bra!' The land-girl turned to him, broad Lancashire.

'An' I can see the top o' thy underpants an' all – and they're mucky!'

Wet lunchtimes, we sometimes shared the back of the army wagon. Embarrassing. The English farmhands discussing the Italians as if they weren't there – really intimately, as if they were cattle. And the Italians discussed us similarly, in Italian. Had there been an interpreter, there'd certainly have been a fight.

One evening I hitched a lift back to the village in the POW truck. Getting off, over the tailgate, I caught myself awkwardly in the crotch. As I lay doubled up in agony on the road, the truck drove off to enormous Italian cheering and laughter. They seemed to think that for once they'd won a victory. Then I realized how much they really hated us.

The German POW was different; a tall thin dignified scare-crow figure in Afrika Korps uniform that grew daily more like a farmhand's gear. He fastened up his trousers with binder-twine, just like they did. He had a little English, very slow, but all the farmhands listened to him patiently. He had owned his own farm in Bavaria, before the war. All he wanted was to get back to it. He was allowed to do any job on the farm, and was allowed to go off on his own. He had shown the farmhands several agricultural tricks they didn't know, and when they were stuck, they would send for him and ask his opinion. He was very loving with animals, especially the dogs. He wouldn't leave any broken thing unmended; spent one lunch-hour mending a drystone wall that had fallen down. He was called 'Fritz' like all German prisoners, and was content to answer to it.

He worked a fiddle with the farmer, who was charged so much an hour for his services. But however hard Fritz worked, he only got five shillings from the POW camp people. So when he'd worked eight hours, he and the farmer would sign his work-card as having worked only four. Then the farmer would give Fritz a packet of fags instead.

Once, when Fritz's camp-lorry broke down and didn't come for him in the evening, he walked back to camp alone. He wished Hitler was dead, so he could go home to his farm. He was the only one allowed inside the farmhouse, for a meal or a bath.

Boy, aged fifteen

1943 INSIDE A POW CAMP

Our regular peregrinations had taken us once round the village. A call at the Co-op joiners-cum-undertakers had resulted in the transfer of a bag of sawdust to the Butchery Dept, with a penny for our trouble. Extra payment on certain days was a glimpse of the odd corpse being well tucked into a coffin.

Our last port of call was the farm, where they'd acquired new pigs. We were both intrigued and disgusted by these creatures wallowing in their filth.

'Let's go to Slater's!'

Two brothers ran the farm; how could their late industrious father have sired such lazy incompetents? At potato-picking time – *if* they'd remembered to sow – they forever had difficulty recruiting labour because of their inability to reach into their money-pockets. But with luck we could avoid them and still see their latest acquisitions . . .

'Who's that?'

'Never seen *him* before.'

'Pity anybody who works for them.' The object of our pity was a lad not much older than us, busy filling a wheelbarrow with the product of the pigs. He nodded, smiled a greeting.

'Is there some new pigs?'

'Yes, in *that* place. Till I have cleaned out *this* place.'

We'd become used to foreign accents invading our village since war began; thought nothing of it. Climbed up, leaned over the wall and saw, to our delight, a sow of gigantic proportions, ministering to her six-strong litter.

'Is she not big?'

'A whopper!'

'She and her little ones arrived yesterday with me.'

'Did you bring them?'

He smiled, shaking his head. 'Me . . . no. I come at same time.'

We were curious . . . but curiosity would have to wait.

'Watch out – Slaters coming!'

We vanished in the opposite direction.

Two days later, having made sure all the village industries were functioning satisfactorily, we returned to view the pigs, making sure the hated brothers were in a distant field.

'Hullo, boys! How are you today?'

Why was he so formal? But his smile was genuine. 'What are your names?'

We told him, adding our nicknames. He didn't seem to understand about nicknames. 'My name is Klaus.'

'That's a funny name!'

'Not in my country.'

'Where's that?'

'Ich bin . . . I am a German.' He looked hard, for our reaction. Two pairs of eyes as wide open as equally open mouths would allow. Where were the jackboots, the swastika, the monocle?

'You're kidding!'

'Kidding? What is that?'

'Go on, talk German, then!'

He smiled, retreated to an adjacent cow-byre.

'Let's go,' said Dennis; no glory in unmasking impostors. Klaus reappeared, jacket over arm. His grin widened as he slipped it on, did a sudden about-turn to display on his back the tell-tale yellow patch.

Our picture of the typical German, conjured up by films, was shattered. How could this young lad be the enemy, who we'd played at killing for four years? Our minds couldn't grasp it. Our friend was now our enemy – or vice-versa? Were tears forming in Dennis's eyes? My heart was beating like mad. I had a lump in my throat.

'Come, see the pigs. I have them in their new place.' We followed, scared to stay but reluctant to go. Wanting to ask so much, but silent, while Klaus, aware of our dilemma, chattered away about the pigs and the names he'd given them.

We visited daily – provided the Slaters weren't in evidence. We supplemented his prison fare with what titbits we could procure. He didn't smoke, but in the camp cigarettes were used as currency. The few Woodbines we managed helped to make his lot easier.

Until the day he didn't appear.

'He might be ill.'

But a week elapsed without a sign.

'Shall we ask the Slaters?'

'Mebbe they've murdered him and hidden the body?'

Knowing the Slaters, I didn't doubt the possibility but ... 'Let's go down the camp and try and see him.'

The camp entrance was separated from the church by the graveyard. The gate had been replaced by a rickety contraption of barbed wire. Inside was a lone sentry-box. Beyond, two rows of huts. We passed by, uncertain, recrossed the road.

'We've come this far – let's ask!'

But what to say ...? We approached the sentry. Rifle in hand, he was shuffling from foot to foot; glanced through the wire, glad of this slight diversion.

'Can we see Klaus Shuster?'

It shook him. 'A prisoner? What you want one of the prisoners for?'

'Got a message for him,' Dennis offered.

'What kind of message? Who from?' He was getting too nosy; we couldn't cope. We tried pleading. 'We've *got* to see him!'

His duty was to stop prisoners getting out; he couldn't cope with people trying to get in. 'Wait here!'

We stood, only waiting for each other to turn tail.

'What's this then, lads?' The voice, loud and strong, belied the tiny man now accompanying the sentry. We stumbled explanations, together and separately. How could a man hardly bigger than us have attained the exalted rank of sergeant? But he listened, not unkindly.

'Do we know him, Jack?'

The sentry shook his head.

'Well, lads, we've got a problem. We don't know the feller you want. You're not supposed to be here, you know!'

I pointed vaguely and desperately to the huts on the left. 'He's just in that hut there, he told us.'

We'd never understand his reasons. He mumbled something to the sentry. The sentry took a keen interest in some far distant object in the opposite direction. The sergeant glanced up and down the road, placed one foot on the lowest strand of barbed wire, and raised the higher one. 'Quick!'

We were in.

'You've got ten minutes. Never seen you, don't know you, and if I catch you I'll kick your arses.'

We had no idea what hut Klaus was in.

A POW appeared at the door of the first hut. Called to us. We didn't understand a word.

'Klaus Shuster?'

He made some reply, disappeared inside. We waited. But the door remained tight shut.

'Let's go home' said Dennis. But we moved along to another open door, and an elderly prisoner with ruddy complexion.

'Klaus Shuster, bitte?'

With a surprised smile, and a pat on the head, he pointed to the hut opposite. We gave him our best 'Danke gute!'

He said something as we retreated; we hadn't a clue.

Hubbub from the hut. We knocked. 'They can't hear us – there's another door inside.' The second door was ajar.

'Go on, knock!'

'You. I asked the soldier on the gate.'

Dennis rapped lightly.

'That's no good – like this!' My puny fists pounded the door, which swung open to disclose an ill-lit, fuggy-atmosphered mass of humanity. The nearest was sitting darning a large grey sock. He looked up, astounded.

'K – K – Klaus Shuster?'

Tall, lank blond hair, blue eyes. It was lucky we understood little German, for his face contorted as he swore, before abruptly turning his back.

The whole room went still. Two lines of faces, gazing down at us from the rows of bunks.

An older man spoke to the blond – perhaps admonished him. Then called down the hut 'Klaus, kommen sie hier.' He pointed to the far end. Through fug and fear, we couldn't recognize our friend, but headed down the room. The centre aisle was clear, apart from two iron stoves. The heat from the stoves and the packed humanity couldn't dispel the cold fear that gripped us, as a heavily built figure leapt from his top bunk to block our way. Between his teeth he muttered something that wasn't friendly.

We stood rooted. He continued to stand threateningly before us, till a companion took him by the arm and drew him back.

'Kinder! – Children!'

From the far end, a familiar figure appeared. Klaus, arms protectively around us, led us to his bunk.

The older man in the bunk above was introduced as Sep. The younger man next door was Vitus. We'd heard about Sep and Vitus. We asked Klaus about the blond, and the thick-set man. They, and one or two more, were glaring in our direction.

'Do not let them trouble you. They do not like the English – they do not like anyone.'

Vitus added quietly: 'They are Nazis.'

'They are few,' said Klaus. 'Most are good, very good, men. No one will allow you to be harmed.'

Our fears disappeared. We could now relish the idea of being in a P O W camp, right in the middle of our enemies.

Klaus told us the Slaters had disagreed with the authorities, as they did with everyone. He'd been transferred to a larger farm, with Sep and Vitus. No facilities existed for post between prisoners and the civilian population, so he couldn't let us know.

Our ten minutes were up. How could we evade the English sergeant? We didn't want to test his veiled threat to kick our arses . . .

'Don't worry,' said Klaus. 'There is a secret way out of the camp.'

Behind the huts, out of sight of the road, the field was only surrounded by a hedge and fence, relics from 1939. And although the gate was festooned with barbed wire, to reassure civilians, the sides and rear were not.

We were proud to be the first civilians to enter the camp (doctors and clergy didn't count). Only later, Klaus disclosed we'd been pipped at the post by a girl not much older than ourselves. We knew her; but all she would say was that she hadn't entered by the gate, like us, and that her visits were for a vastly different purpose . . .

We found a gap in the hedge. Down the narrow lane to meet the main street, and the road for home.

Boy, north-east

CHAPTER 16

D-DAY

THE MOST CRITICAL DAY

Dearest Mummy,

Can hardly contain myself now the invasion has started and I want to congratulate Daddy. We had the RAF march-past today and can see the planes roaring over and hear the guns. Could you please cut out anything of interest about the invasion and send it? We are going to have regular 'news' here and we are getting jolly excited. Hooray for Churchill, but it's not all glorious. We are praying hard. Please write.

Best of love, Jill

I put my picture of Daddy up last night, and everyone going past had to salute it ... great fun. One of the other girls' father is also in the RAF.

Today, I have the urge to write about the most critical and moving day of our history. At last, after the dark anxious days we can hit back, while thousands of our troops are moving into action across the Channel. 'The End of the Beginning' at least! But how many anxious mothers are thinking of their sons who might never return but are proud to be the first to suffer in the great and glorious cause of the invasion which means peace. The world goes on as usual, as it must, but in everyone's heart there is a conscious feeling of victory but we must never forget the men who are fighting for us and their country. The British Lion is certainly very awake and his jaws are crushing the mighty weight of the German war machine. In the quietness of the chapel we pray for the valiant men. The Tommies who loved

Mulberry, the artificial harbour made of sunken ships: there was a pipeline called 'Pluto' (Petroleum Line Under the Ocean) laid right across the English Channel to pump fuel-oil to France. D-Day to us was the beginning of technical miracles: some troops were said to have ball-point pens that could write under water ...

213

peace but can move in anger to war for their country and loved ones.

Girl, aged fifteen, Hampshire

MY COUSIN

My cousin George Freeman was killed in Normandy on D-Day Plus 2. He was very little, so they made him into a tank gunner, because there's not much room in a tank turret. His tank commander wrote to my Aunt Edith, saying that their tank was hit by a shell in a tank-duel with Panzers. He and my cousin got out quick, as the tank was starting to 'brew up' and about to explode. The last time he saw my cousin, he was running for cover.

I know what happened; in a tank battle, they gun down the crew escaping from a brewing-up tank, so they don't live to drive another tank. Both sides do it. Probably the Panzer gunner did it without giving it a thought, like spraying roses for greenfly.

I only ever really talked to my cousin once, because my Aunt Edith had so many kids that when you went to their house, you could never tell which was which. At tea-time, the grown-ups had to eat first, and the kids second, as there wasn't enough room at the table. This always made me feel deeply insulted ...

But once George came to tea with me alone. He was Aunt Edith's favourite, the clever one, who had a job in an office. He came beautifully turned out (in contrast with the rest) and was very quiet and had beautiful manners. Although he was three years older than me, he let me organize all the games we played. When he saw our tea-table, even in the war, his eyes went like saucers, and he ate an awful lot, but very slowly and politely. When he went he shook hands with us, and thanked us for having him. He looked like he'd been in the Kingdom of Heaven.

I thought about him a lot, after he was killed. He was only eighteen, and his life seemed to have hardly started. It seemed he might as well never have been. I thought about Aunt Edith; she had about eight more kids, but he was the favourite.

Boy, aged fourteen, Tyneside

LIBERATION

I remember waking up on 9 September 1944 to a lot of noise and people shouting. Looking out of the window towards a nearby airfield, I saw the most wonderful sight – the sky was full of parachutes. Everyone was crying and laughing at the same time and shouting 'It's the Tommies!'

I remember going into town on my way to work and seeing tanks and lorries full of British soldiers – people at the roadside waving Dutch flags and sometimes grabbing hold of a soldier and hugging and thanking him.

I remember while watching this parade a message was passed saying 'The Germans are coming back.' The streets cleared and everyone ran for shelter as fast as they could. Remembering the German threat, that their last bombs would be for Eindhoven. True to their word, they bombed the town that night. Many people were killed and buildings destroyed. Our little air-raid shelter, only big enough for five people, was packed full with ten people including children. My sister was hanging halfway outside and warned us to 'duck' when she saw the bombs falling from the planes. We all ducked as much as the room we were allowed, and when the impact of the explosions rocked our house and shelter, we thought our last hour had come.

I remember the day after this bombardment the people of our part of town lost all control of themselves. Their hatred, so long stifled, had now free range, and was turned towards the women and girls who had been friendly with the Germans. The women were rounded up and all their hair was shaved from their heads. On top of this bald head a swastika was painted, so everyone could recognize them as traitors. The screams of the women were awful. And no matter how hard the coming winter weather, no woman would wear a hat or a headscarf. Just to show they had been true to Holland.

I remember walking into an office, which had been taken over by the British Army, and meeting for the first time the man who was to become my husband. But that is another story.

Girl, aged eighteen, Eindhoven

CHAPTER 17 FLYING BOMBS AND V2s

1944 FLYING BOMBS

On 16 June we woke early in our dormitories to hear a peculiar sound in the sky – a phut, phut – with machine-gun fire. Eventually it was announced that the long-awaited Flying Bomb offensive had started. We became very blasé with these little jet-planes streaking overhead, only making a dive under the table when it cut out, and there was that long ominous pause before it crashed and exploded. One sunny afternoon, before the A A gunners, planes and barrage balloons had sorted themselves out, we had the remarkable sight of a Hawker Tempest chasing one of the buzz-bombs straight down the playing-field firing cannon-shell at it. Regrettably the V1 crashed on a residential area beyond Epsom. The school authorities became worried about the constant interruption, so we were sent home, except for those taking exams, many of whom did far better than expected, since allowances were made for their having to dive under the desks several times during each exam.

Boy, aged sixteen, Sussex

1944 V 2s

The awful moment of silence when the putt-putting engine cut out, and you counted, waiting for the bang. June 1944.

On 8 September I was standing in our lounge when the windows shook violently. First accounts said a gasometer had exploded, but eventually censors released the news that the first of the V 2 rockets had landed at Chiswick. Fortunately Putney was spared the devastation caused by these 'whispering giants' – sometimes one could just hear the rush of air before the explosion. But by the time the last rocket fell on Orpington on 27 March 1945, 2,700 people had been killed and 6,500 seriously injured. While less accurate than the Flying Bomb, it was more deadly, leaving a crater 30 ft. deep.

Boy, aged sixteen, Sussex

1944 RESCUE WORK

The terrace had fallen like a pack of cards. These were terraced houses (with an area at the front), reached by a bridge to the front door, one storey up. This front wall was supporting the remaining structure. The entire back walls had collapsed. The floors therefore hung down on one another.

One family, husband, wife and two girls, had taken shelter that night (at the back) when the husband returned to make tea. He heard the bomb approaching and ran to the front of his house to see where it went. It struck the back of his house, completely destroying it, leaving him unhurt on the remains of the small concrete bridge to his front door. Unfortunately his good fortune was not shared by his family. We found them all dead from blast in their Anderson shelter. The demented husband was taken to hospital for sedation.

The remaining houses in the terrace had to be searched. A check on the shelters indicated approximately four people unaccounted for. The floors had to be carefully jacked-up, and holes made through each, to enable us to enter and search. As I was young and slim, I was asked to go in. The first house offered nothing. We moved next door. A hole was made and I slid in with my torch. Up ahead I could hear a moan and I cleared a way through each floor. I uncovered a middle-aged woman lying on a sofa. She was still alive and apparently unhurt, although her body was supporting the timbers above. Beside her, on the floor and free of debris, lay her sister. She was dead. I signalled the rescue squad and withdrew. They were able to extricate them, the first going to the hospital, the second to the mortuary.

The next house I slid into, the situation was similar. In this one I found a young woman crouching over her child. Both were dead, though the child was still warm, indicating that the mother's protective instinct had saved the child from the blast, only for it to suffocate.

Boy, aged sixteen, London

1944 RUNNING REPAIRS

Dad said he would have a go at the upstairs ceiling tomorrow, and we retired exhausted.

The next day dawned bright and hot. We opened those window-frames that were openable, and Dad mounted the step-ladder in the middle bedroom. Placing both hands to the centre of the ceiling he gently eased the whole area back to the rafters. Having achieved this, he released one hand to locate a nail to hammer in and secure.

Suddenly there was a roar and the whole ceiling collapsed, filling the room with dust and debris, which billowed through the window apertures to envelop the house completely.

Neighbours came running, thinking another bomb may have fallen. When the dust cleared, I was able to see my father still standing on the step-ladder and still holding a small piece of ceiling in place. He was completely covered with dust, looking like a statue. I'm afraid that we found it absolutely hilarious, a complete break to the tension we were all subject to. We fell about laughing, much to my father's annoyance, until he too saw the funny side of the incident.

Boy, aged seventeen, London

1944 AFTER THE DOODLEBUG

Overhead cables had fallen across the barbed wire and I received a nasty shock on contact.

All around were bits of the girls to whom I had waved so often. Military personnel arrived with large baskets, into which they placed the remains. It was a fearful sight which filled me with rage at such senseless slaughter.

The tension was relieved when a milkman with his horse and float came jogging up. Seeing the road blocked by debris, he attempted to turn his vehicle too sharply and in doing so turned the cart over. Milk bottles were rolling in all directions and milk flowed into the gutters. Many of the rescuers left their life-saving task amongst the ruins to try to retrieve this foolish man's load. Some people have funny priorities.

Boy, aged seventeen, London

1944 FLYING BOMB

In the evenings I sometimes rode my bike to the top of Plum Lane, where I could view most of east and south-east London. From this point of view it was possible to see the flight-patterns of the bombs and where they fell. It was a macabre sight, knowing that when the mushroom cloud of smoke came up people were dying in horrible circumstances. I never felt myself at risk – the optimism of youth, no doubt!

Once, on returning along Red Road on a day when there was a low cloud base, I was suddenly confronted with a flying bomb coming straight at me through the clouds. It happened so quickly I was unable to get off my bike before it exploded in an allotment 50 yards away. I was thrown through the air to land further up the road from my bike. The soft earth of the allotment had saved me, as the blast was mainly upward. I was dazed and suffered some concussion.

Boy, aged seventeen, London

1945 THE END OF THE FLYING BOMBS

As the new year 1945 progressed, the attacks diminished. People came to ignore the occasional explosion.

I recall one day seeing a vapour trail cross the sky, followed shortly by a double bang. That rocket, I was to learn, fell behind Selfridges in London.

Another memory was of a rocket which had failed to explode and was stuck in a garden in Abbey Wood like a gigantic dart.

People you knew were no longer around. Schoolfriends had been killed. Familiar buildings had been destroyed.

Things started to return to normal. Repairs were being made to houses. Glass was being put back into window-frames, ceilings were being replaced, new doors and casements fitted. Houses began to recover their pre-war look.

However, with this relaxation came the return of the Englishman's reserve and isolation. People who had shared misery and laughter only six months previously now hardly acknowledged each other when they met. This was also felt acutely by the Civil Defence, which had once again become a 'burden on the rate-payer'.

Our armies were streaming across Europe and 'our war' seemed to be nearly over.

I regret the Civil Defence organization had to die; it just faded away. Although it was officially stood down on 8 May 1945, it was by that time virtually non-existent. All the local wardens were unpaid volunteers, except two lady wardens paid by the council. They were exhausted by the demands made on them over previous years and would not report when there was no likelihood of their being needed.

Boy, aged seventeen, London

3-POWER ANNOUNCEMENT TO-DAY; BUT BRITAIN KNEW LAST NIGHT

VE-DAY—IT'S ALL OVER

All quiet till 9 p.m.—then the London crowds went mad in the West End

By Day ↑
↓ By Night

THE Face of Victory—by day and night : Roadways in and around Piccadilly-circus were jammed nearly solid yesterday afternoon by crowds waiting to hear VE-Day announced. Then they decided not to wait—they began to celebrate. These Daily Mail pictures give you a vivid impression of the great concourse of joy—above by day : on the left, by night. Other scenes—Pages THREE and FOUR.

PM put off the big speech

UNTIL TO-DAY

By WILSON BROADBENT, Diplomatic Correspondent

GERMANY surrendered unconditionally to the Allies yesterday. But there will be no official announcement of victory until 3 p.m. to-day — officially described as V E-Day—when Mr. Churchill will give the news to the world.

He will follow this with an address to the House of Commons, and at 9 p.m. the King will speak to Britain and the Empire.

Mr. Churchill's private car at the House of Commons was last night "wired-up" so that if he wishes he can make his broadcast from there.

To-day's announcement will be made simultaneously in London, Washington, and Moscow. To-day, therefore, is the first of the promised two-days V-holiday for the country.

Broadcasts will also be made by General Eisenhower and Field-Marshals Montgomery and Alexander.

Mr. Churchill's two statements to-day will not affect his intention to broadcast at length on Thursday night, the fifth anniversary of his assumption of the Premiership.

After his statement in the House of Commons, Mr. Churchill will propose the adjournment of business while M.P.s attend a special Service of Thanksgiving at St. Margaret's Church, Westminster. They will then return to the House of Commons and adjourn, and arrange to meet again on Wednesday.

Until shortly before 8 o'clock last night it was fully expected that Mr. Churchill would be able to announce the news that the war was over.

Victory lunch

He had been standing by the microphone from some time after 6 o'clock, and everything was ready for him to break in the normal programmes of the B.B.C.

Earlier in the day he had been speaking on the Transatlantic telephone to Washington, and he also had several calls to Moscow. His object was to obtain an agreed time for releasing the big news.

There was apparently an agreement that there should be simultaneous times for release. Apparently in London it was understood that Monday would be suitable to all concerned.

In anticipation of this important occasion Mr. Churchill gave a special Victory luncheon party at No. 10 Downing-street for the Chiefs of Staff whose health he personally proposed.

After luncheon Mr. Churchill was ready to broadcast, but as neither of Washington's or Moscow's agreed had been received—

It was nearly 8 o'clock when it was learned that both the United States and the Soviet Government were in favour of postponing the formal announcing until this afternoon.

Moscow preferred this course because of certain final formalities connected with the German pact, which will take place to-day. Washington had other reasons which are not yet known. So Mr. Churchill, finding himself in a minority, had to agree.

CZECHS TOLD TO 'SMASH GERMANS'

Czech-controlled radio early to-day appealed to Patriots to man the barricades to attack and smash German positions. Radio declared that "Protector" Frank yesterday made "arrogant" offer to resign and ordered some fire if Czechs would lay down barricades.—Reuter.

TARAKAN NEARLY CUT IN TWO

Manila, Tuesday. — Allies cleared ground east of the main oilfield on Tarakan, off Borneo, and advanced across the island to within a mile and a half of the east shore. Fighting continues for Tarakan town.—B.U.P.

4

U.S. made it VE-Day all the same

Work walk-out

From DON IDDON, Daily Mail Correspondent

New York, Monday.

THIS was VE-Day in the U.S.—official or not.

The celebrations began in New York at breakfast-time, a few minutes after word came from Rheims, France, that Germany had surrendered unconditionally to Britain, the United States, and Russia.

They went on all day despite an avalanche of confused messages, lack of official confirmation, half-denials, and a barrage of rumours that the surrender was a hoax.

The American public, and particularly the New York public, this time was determined that this was the end of the war in Europe, and resolved to commemorate it.

The first reaction and it was the same all over Manhattan was to pop open windows, tear up telephone directories, and hurl paper into the streets.

For hours tons upon tons of ticker tape, torn-up newspapers, envelopes, letters, magazines, and in some instances hats and waste-paper baskets, cascaded down

Jammed roads

Tens of thousands of people abandoned work and rushed into the Times-square area choosing and singing. Motorists blew their hooters, factory whistles shrieked, and in New York Bay ships sounded their sirens.

Bands of Service men and girls paraded the avenues, waving flags, shouting and yelling, planting kisses on strangers, converting it into a ball of holly.

Great silver streamers, tiny flicker of confetti fell down as with we could not go on...

Traffic was completely held in midtown in districts of gridlock taxis, laughing people jammed roads uptown. Over the streets of gridlock traffic the big crowds of hilarious men, women and women

At first day, ration fed to Mayor La Guardia attempted to curb the jubilation.

Over the radio came a reminder that there are roving crowds that it was more a day which had declared was it. In Europe and the people out of the...

Daily Mail

IN accordance with the announcement of the Government that war workers generally should enjoy a day's holiday following the announcement in Europe, The Daily Mail, in common with other London morning newspapers, will not be published on Thursday.

The war still goes on here—

PRAGUE BOMBED AS SS SHOOT CZECH CIVILIANS

GERMAN bombs are falling on Prague for the first time as the war in Europe enters its last hours. In defiance of surrender orders, German forces in Czecho-Slovakia are fighting on. They are venting their last spite on the Czechs, shooting them down ruthlessly in the streets of the capital.

Refugees from Prague who have reached Allied-controlled Pilsen say that, in many cases, the S.S. went through the city desiring people out of their houses into the streets.

And when other S.S. men massed in concentration took their gun at the crowds. One refugee told how little escaped and was made...

Thus the SS are completely out of hand is indicated in a broadcast by the German commander in Bohemia and Moravia warning the troops to respect international law.

'Evil Hitler'

A Czech Spitfire squadron of formations of large aircraft escorting Czech ground troops, have left Britain for Czecho-Slovakia.

Broadcasting from London last night, Dr. Hubert Hipka, Czechoslovak Minister of Foreign Trade, said that his bailing on after the general nightfall in the German-controlled areas between the line out which be dealt with a...

Asked if Hitler was same, Dr. Schacht said "In some things no others he is a crook..."

Someone suggested to a gentle and Schacht said "Yes, an evil..." and Schacht said "an evil and sadistic one to..."

Pilsen kisses

Pilsen, Monday.

LIEUT-GENERAL MAJEWSKI commanding the German garrison...

V E WEATHER

Spell of finer weather yesterday. Victory weather, with hours of sunshine. Day temperature, rising.

BACK-PAGE—Col. EIGHT

SYMBOL of the mood of London : lamp-post, waves a flag above the thin man, at the top of a crowds—Daily Mail picture.

Beacon chain begun by Piccadilly's bonfires

By GUY RAMSEY

LONDON, dead from six until nine, suddenly broke into victory life last night. Suddenly, spontaneously, deliriously. The people of London, denied VE-Day officially, held their own jubilation. "VE-Day may be to-morrow," they said, "but the war is over to-night." Bonfires blazed from Piccadilly to Wapping.

The sky once lit by the glare of the blitz shone red with the Victory glow. The last trains departed from the West End unregarded. The pent-up spirits of the throng, the polyglot throng that is London in war-time, burst out, and by 11 o'clock the capital was ablaze with enthusiasm.

Processions formed out of nowhere, disintegrating for no reason, to re-form somewhere else. Waving flags, marching in step, with linked arms or half-embraced, the people strode down the great thoroughfares—Piccadilly, Regent-street, the Mall, to the portals of Buckingham Palace.

They marched and counter-marched so as not to get too far from the centre. And from them, in harmony and discord, rose song. The songs of the last war, the songs of a century ago. The songs of the beginning of this war—"Roll out the Barrel" and "Tipperary"; "Ilkla Moor" and "Loch Lomond"; "Bless 'em All" and "Pack Up Your Troubles."

ROCKETS AND SONGS

Rockets—found no-one knows where, set-off by no-one knows whom—streaked into the sky, exploding not in death but a burst of scarlet fire. A pile of straw filled with thunder-flashes salvaged from some military dump spurted and exploded near Leicester-square.

Every car that challenged the milling, moiling throng was submerged in humanity. They climbed on the running-boards, on the bonnet, on the roof. They hammered on the panels. They shouted and sang.

Against the drumming on metal came the clash of cymbals, improvised out of dustbin lids. The dustbin itself was a football for an impromptu Rugger scrum. Rubbling, exploding with gaiety, the people matheked. Headlights silhouetted couples kissing, couples cheering, couples waving flags.

Every cornice, every lamp-post was scaled. Americans marched with A.T.S. girls in civvies, fresh from their work benches, ran by the side of battle-dressed

Continued in Back Page, Col. 6

SCHACHT SAVED BY 'FIFTH'

Niemoller, too

Daily Mail Special Correspondent

ALLIES H.Q., Italy, Monday.

SOME of the most famous victims of Nazi-ism have been rescued by the Fifth Army from the Prager Wildsee prison camp, near Oblacao, Italy.

Among them was Pastor Niemoller, head of the German Confessional Church, whose defiance of Hitler led to a seven years' incarceration in concentration camps.

A few hours after his release Pastor Niemoller held a service in the lounge of a hotel.

His text was the words of Isaiah:

"For the mountains shall depart, and the hills be removed; but my kindness shall not depart from thee; neither shall the covenant of my peace be removed, saith the Lord that hath mercy on thee."

In all, the Fifth Army saved 126 hostages, including Dr. Schuschnigg, former Chancellor of Austria, who during the week-end was strenuously reported to have been murdered.

Dr. Schuschnigg's wife was also saved. M. Leon Blum, former Socialist Premier of France, and his wife, were also freed.

GOEBBELS' BODY IN A SHELTER

GOEBBELS, the German Propaganda Minister, his wife, and five children have been found dead in Berlin.

Moscow says that their bodies were found in an air-raid shelter near the Reichstag, and it has been established that all died of poisoning.

No trace has been found of the bodies of Hitler or Göring.

There was speculation in London last night whether the Nazi leaders may have fled to a place of hiding.

It was pointed out, however, that their bodies may have been destroyed in the wreckage of the burning Chancellery or some other building.

Moscow radio last night reported, says B.U.P. that troops had penetrated deep into an underground fortress in the basement of Hitler's Chancellery.

"Smoke is pouring from an unexplored depth into which we had been unable to penetrate," said the radio.

MONTY MEETS ROKOSSOVSKY

4 toasts at lunch

TWENTY-FIRST ARMY GROUP, Monday.— Field-Marshal Montgomery lunched to-day with Marshal Konstantin Rokossovsky at Wismar.

Toasts were drunk to the Allied armies, Mr. Churchill, Marshal Stalin, and President Truman.—Reuter.

Home by searchlight

There will be a searchlight display by the A.A. over Central London and London suburbs on VE-Night, from 11.15 p.m. to 12.15 a.m. and again on the next night at the same time.

ARRESTED POLES MAY BE TRIED BY LUBLIN

LUBLIN radio said yesterday that the Polish Provisional Government may demand that the 16 Poles arrested by the Russians be tried both in Warsaw and Moscow for high treason.

The radio said : Public opinion in Poland has received, with indignation the news of the arrest of Polish officials and his accomplices who were accused of carrying out a contrary activities against the Red Army.

Because the criminal activities against the Red Army and his accomplices were also directed against the re-

been Polish State. It constitutes high treason.

The Provisional Government considers the right to demand that the Okulicki and his accomplices be called over to the Polish authorities to be indicted in the courts of the Republic as well.

Mr. Mikolajczyk, former Deputy Prime Minister in London, has expressed yesterday that he is proceeding a statement on the arrests.

He said that the arrested men cannot be accused of high treason against the Soviet forces, as they were known persons of Polish-Soviet understanding.

CHAPTER 18 VICTORY!

HER MAJESTY THE QUEEN: ONE OF THE MOST MEMORABLE NIGHTS OF MY LIFE

I remember the thrill and relief after the previous day's waiting for the Prime Minister's announcement of the end of the War in Europe. My parents went out on the balcony in response to the huge crowds outside. I think we went on the balcony nearly every hour, six times, and then when the excitement of the floodlights being switched on got through to us, my sister and I realized we couldn't see what the crowds were enjoying. My mother had put her tiara on for the occasion, so we asked my parents if we could go out and see for ourselves. I remember we were terrified of being recognized, so I pulled my uniform cap well down over my eyes. A grenadier officer amongst our party of about sixteen people said he refused to be seen in the company of another officer improperly dressed, so I had to put my cap on normally. We cheered the King and Queen on the balcony and then walked miles through the streets. I remember lines of un-known people linking arms and walking down Whitehall, all of us just swept along on a tide of happiness and relief. I remember the amazement of my cousin, just back from four and a half years in a Prisoner of War camp, walking freely with his family in the friendly throng. And I also remember when someone exchanged hats with a Dutch sailor, the poor man coming along with us in order to get his cap back. After crossing Green Park we stood outside and shouted 'We want the King', and we were successful in seeing my parents on the balcony, having cheated slightly because we sent a message into the house to say we were waiting outside. I think it was one of the most memorable nights of my life.

The Queen talking to Godfrey Talbot, broadcast in a BBC radio documentary The Way We Were, *transmitted on Radio 4, 8 May 1985*

V E DAY

Our street had a great big party and everyone painted their houses red, white and blue. We had nice things to eat, even a cake.

My Aunty Al got her piano out and played in the street and everyone was dancing and singing. The party went on all through the night. Everybody had a great time. In school next day we all got an apple from Canada each; it was beautiful, big and red.

Girl, aged six, Liverpool

DANCING IN THE STREET

We had a dance in the street. I was in great demand, being fifteen and big, and able to dance. It felt quite delightfully wicked, dancing with all the young wives of the soldiers, sailors and airmen, who weren't there. It was hot, and they only wore thin dresses, and they danced very freely that night, and didn't seem to care.

There was a big bonfire, afterwards. I got the whole incendiary bomb, that I'd kept all during the war, and threw it on the bonfire, but it still didn't go off.

Boy, aged fifteen, Tyneside

V E NIGHT IN EDINBURGH

On V E night my father was still away in the Army. My mother said 'C'mon, let's go riding on the tram.' We went right across Edinburgh to Corstophine for 1d. There were people climbing up the outside of the tram – you couldn't see out of the windows, it was smothered in drunks. Every vehicle moving was covered with people drinking from bottles. Even high up on the trams, near the sparkling electric high-tension wires. Dozens of American sailors with a girl on each arm. You went up to them and said 'Got any gum, chum?' They always gave you some; their blouses were full of packets of gum.

Boy, aged ten

Australians, girls and Americans — for once in peaceful proximity. The 'turban' was still with us (and would be for some years), the legs are bare (but covered with 'liquid stockings' — brownish stain) and the novelty-vendors must have been getting their paper hats ready before Adolf finally killed himself.

A BONFIRE

My grandmother had five sons coming home, who she called the Royals, as they were in the Royal Navy, Royal Air Force and Royal Liverpool Regiment. She said she would have a bonfire. She did have one, and she was dancing all round it until she found that my grandfather had put all her furniture on the bonfire.

Girl, aged eleven, Liverpool

'UP WEST'

I was staying with a maiden aunt in London and was taken 'up West' with many thousand other, cheering, laughing, crying, singing people. I had never seen anything like it, and so was totally unprepared for a bear-hug from an American soldier, who lifted me right off my feet and swung me round, and landed me a smacking kiss. Hallelujah!

Later, we gathered outside Buckingham Palace. Who cares about rain? We began to chant 'We want the King! We want the King!'

I was yelling down the ear of a Canadian soldier. He turned to me. 'Some of us don't,' he said.

'What you want to come here for, then?' I asked.

He shrugged and made no reply, just went on standing in the rain.

Girl, aged fourteen, London

FATHER'S RETURN

I went to Lime Street Station to meet 'The Picture on the Wall'.

Because the only thing I had seen of my Dad was the photo that hung on the wall. And when I played tig and ran across the tables, I always felt guilty in front of that picture.

Boy, Liverpool

WAR CRIMINALS

They are going to try old Fatty Goering and Rudolf Hess too, as war criminals. All the ones who didn't kill themselves in May, before the surrender. It doesn't seem fair. All the wicked ones *killed* themselves – Himmler, Hitler, Goebbels. Old Fatty Goering was only a laugh – he was in the *Beano* and the *Dandy* – no one ever took him seriously. Hess flew to this country, at the risk of his own life, to try for peace. They wouldn't even *talk* to him. Was that *his* fault? And poor old Lord Haw-Haw, too. I mean, old Haw-Haw kept us laughing, in the worst times of the war. You might as well try Tommy Handley as a war criminal and traitor. Besides, Haw-Haw can't be a traitor to the British, he was an American citizen, and broadcast when America wasn't even at war . . .

We had a debate about war criminals in the Sixth Form and they were all being so pious and righteous – it made me sick. So I got up and really let loose. What about *our* war criminals? What about Butcher Harris of Bomber Command, who burnt 100,000 women and children alive, in the Hamburg Fire-typhoon? What about Churchill and Truman, who atom-bombed Hiroshima and Nagasaki? They were all war criminals too. But I suppose you only get tried as a war criminal if you're on the losing side. Otherwise you are a hero!

I expected to get slammed to hell by the rest of the class. But one or two more spoke up the same way, and there was a lot of clapping, and then suddenly a lot of excitement and cheering, and we passed a motion to have Churchill and Roosevelt and

This one, I came back to again and again. The whole story was there. It was obvious the Australian had been shot down a long time before, because of his beard and painful thinness. Because one couldn't see his face, one looked at his body harder, and knew so much about him. In spite of living in the jungle with the natives, he had kept his beard and uniform neat. And he has a look of gentle decency, of coming to terms with danger, suffering and death. Even something Christlike about him . . . The tribesmen look upset: they must have learnt to love him.

The guards holding the tribesmen back are enjoying the sport. Britishers might do this kind of thing to foxes, but not to humans.

The executioner – puny, strutting, myopic, inferior – killing a helpless man . . . cheating again. This was not an official Japanese war photograph, but a holiday snapshot found in a dead soldier's wallet. A record of an enjoyable event, like our lads being photographed in a rickshaw in front of the Taj Mahal. I would sit there and stare at it, and hate for hours.

The picture was published in May 1945. It became a powerful propaganda weapon in the last days of the war, and helped make the dropping of the atomic bombs seem more acceptable.

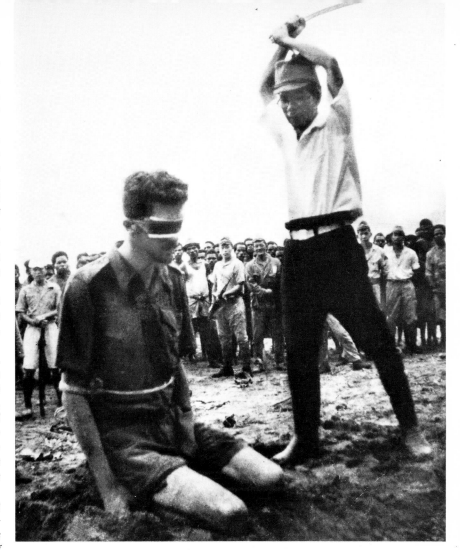

Truman and Harris tried as war criminals. Somebody said Harris would say he was only obeying orders.

Old Puggie Anderson, our English teacher, gave me a funny look. Then he said it was about time I went to university, because I had this need to discuss.

Boy, aged sixteen, Tyneside

THE JAPANESE

We started off despising the Japanese; we thought we'd beat them easy. My father would only buy British goods, or German; even in the war, he bought me German toys because they were 'well made'. Everything else was 'foreign rubbish' and worst of all was 'Japanese rubbish'. He once bought a Japanese lighter for a shilling. It worked twice, then broke; I'll never forget the gesture of disgust with which he threw it in the fire. We thought the Japanese fighter-planes' wings would fall off; we thought their fleet would sink in the first storm.

Inexplicably, they didn't.

The Japs won, in the jungles of Malaya. But that was because they could climb in the trees, like the monkeys they practically were. They ran about in brainless yellow hordes, like ants. They were all exactly the same, tiny, bald, yellow, with spectacles, thin moustaches and buck-teeth. They didn't need *supplies* like real men, they could live on beetles and nuts. And they committed atrocities - disembowelled their prisoners and staked them out for the ants to eat; raped every female in sight; cut steaks from the sides of living water buffalo, which staggered about, bleeding.

And then came the Aleutian campaign, when they committed suicide in huge numbers, rather than be taken prisoner; holding a hand-grenade to their bellies, then pulling out the pin.

I mean, we knew the Nazis were nasty, but in the war we were always on the lookout for the Good German ... the fighter ace, shot down and entertained to dinner in the local RAF Officers' Mess. The compassionate U-boat commander; the shot-down bomber-gunner who was no more than a young lad, and was given a cup of tea. Nobody ever looked for a good Jap. Tolkien was writing 'The Lord of the Rings' then, and if you want to know how we saw the Japs, we saw them as Orcs. Or rats, or flies ... If we'd have had an aerosol spray that killed Japs, we'd have killed the lot.

And of course, we had. When the atomic bombs were dropped on Hiroshima and Nagasaki, we stood up in the cinema and cheered our heads off. We were not just proud, we were deeply and vilely satisfied ... like eating a hot meat pie.

Boy, Tyneside

THE ONE THAT GOT AWAY

The most fantastic thing that any Children of the Blitz got up to was the Battle of Barmouth. The battle lasted thirty-eight hours, and 5,000 rounds of live ammunition were fired. By three Welsh thirteen-year-olds, at a variety of British soldiers. At one point 1,800 troops were involved, hunting down the teenage desperadoes on the slopes of Cader Idris. It is a blessing that no one was killed. Churchill called for the children to be tried for attempted murder. Herbert Morrison, the Home Secretary, managed to placate him.

The only trouble is that it was so big, fantastic and frightening in its implications, that no one will talk about it. The affair came to my notice first in the *Sunday Express* of 20 February 1944.

3 BOYS AND A PLATOON OF MARINES

With three rifles and 400 rounds of 0.22 ammunition, three boys aged 12 to 14 defied a platoon of marines 36 strong, led by two subalterns, in the Welsh Mountains round Cader Idris.

For two days and nights they carried out their own guerrilla warfare, only surrendering under the protection of a white flag when reduced to two rounds of ammunition.

On Thursday the boys broke into the armoury of a camp at Barmouth. Three rifles and all the ammunition were taken. Soon the theft was discovered and a hue and cry started.

The lieutenant-quartermaster was recalled from leave, and the brigadier's batman sent after the young desperadoes.

When bullets started whizzing round his head, he decided that reinforcements were needed and went back for the regimental police.

They in turn retired in the face of superior enemy fire and the National Fire Service were called out. They gave up.

The boys were all night on the mountain and shot two fowls belonging to a local poultry-keeper. They then went to a disused mine in the mountains and dug themselves in.

On Friday, a platoon of marines, 36 strong with two subalterns, set out on the chase. They tracked the boys down and the bullets began flying again. The platoon got under cover and prepared to attack. Firing blank cartridges, they made a frontal assault on the boys' position, but had to retreat. Reinforcements were sent for, and a captain came to supervise.

Ammunition was running low and the boys flew a white flag. Out they came, with just two rounds, but without the rifles, which have not been found yet.

The three were marched back to their home town, under an escort of eight marines.

The boys were placed 'under restriction' at their homes, but last night went to the local cinema, feted by all the boys in the neighbourhood.

Of course, I wanted to know more. I wrote to the Director of the Royal Marines, and I appealed for witnesses in the local Barmouth newspaper. The Marines were charming, and put the affair in context. Barmouth has fine sands, and a lot of empty hillside behind. As D-Day approached, the whole area became one massive armed camp, a training-ground for D-Day 'rear-echelons' like landing-craft crews, beach-masters and also officer cadets. The Royal Marines had two camps, 'Iceland' and 'Crete'. There was also an airfield, an aircraft strafing and bombing range, street-fighting training areas and an ordnance factory. The little town of Barmouth was engulfed in this mass of military, but not evacuated of civilians. With civilians actually inside the camp, security does not seem to have been taken seriously. There was also local Welsh resentment. As Matthew Little of the Royal Marines Museum wrote, 'There could well have been some ill-feeling in the community as part of "Crete" camp was made up of requisitioned houses at the north end of the river bridge; a factor that may have made some grounds for resentment in a disrupted community.' It was 'Crete' camp where the trouble started.

What is also clear, from the account of the *Express* reporter who attended the boys' trial, is the panic among both civil and military authorities as the boys resolved themselves from mere thieves into children who had gone berserk with deadly weapons, and might do *anything*. It is little wonder that in the final battle, the two subalterns were so overcome with the dilemma of capturing the children unharmed, without risking the lives of their own men, that a captain had to be summoned. Had either a child or a marine been killed or wounded in that traditionally Welsh Nationalist area, the results would have been appalling. Yet captured they had to be; not only were they making arseholes of a brigade of the British Forces; the fusillades of rifle-fire coming down the hillside had convinced the citizens of Barmouth that German paratroops had landed, and the town was on the verge of panic.

Afterwards, there must have been the father and mother of a court of inquiry, let alone a civilian trial and several courts martial. But the Marines state the records have been 'destroyed'.

However, they obligingly sent a photocopy of the *Sunday People* of 27 April 1975. The War Cabinet papers for March 1944 had just then been released, and reporter David Jack was on to a correspondence between Winston Churchill and the Home Secretary, Herbert Morrison, on this very topic.

Winston Churchill, angry about 'this extraordinary affair', wrote 'The point is, did the boys fire with bullets on the Marines? If they did, the case is grave and they should be charged with attempted murder. We really cannot have the young hooligans setting upon the Royal Marines with bullets.'

After extensive inquiries, Morrison managed to placate the fearsome old lion.

'There is no evidence that the boys shot intentionally at the Marines or anybody else. The only living things among the various targets selected by the high-spirited youngsters were some chickens.' Two chickens died.

David Jack actually ran the three desperadoes to earth in 1975, and wrote an article treating the whole thing as a harmless giggle. I will return to his stuff later.

Meanwhile, my inquiries in the Barmouth local paper began to result in what I can only call a minor Welsh Watergate Scandal. People kept writing me anonymous postcards saying cryptically 'If you want to know the truth, ring this number'! Or, 'Old so-and-so, who lives at so-and-so, could tell you a thing or two.' The nickname 'Chicago' kept being mentioned; apparently, the leader of the three boys has been known since the shoot-out as 'Chicago' to the present day. When I rang numbers, or wrote letters, nobody was saying anything; only recommending that I ring their aunty's husband, who had moved to Cornwall ... it was all very Welsh. Then a Welshman came on the line to my wife, when I was out, threatening all kinds of awful things if I wrote a *word*. She was twenty minutes calming him down, and couldn't understand half what he was talking about, but apparently he made out he was one of the three boys involved . . .

But my Watergate had a Deep Throat too. Another Welsh voice, making out he was one of the three involved, and I was inclined to believe him, from internal evidence. He promised to write it all down for me, but inexplicably never did so . . . Luckily, I took notes verbatim at the time. This is what Deep Throat *said*.

We were resentful. Barmouth had been a peaceful little town before the war. Then we had two invasions – first an invasion of evacuees from Liverpool, then an invasion of English soldiers, making us talk English instead of our own language.

We watched; we knew everything that moved – the ammunition trains from the ordnance factory. If we'd been – known – a Fifth columnist, we could have told him everything.

We had nothing to do all day but watch them. By the end we knew how to use, fire and strip a sixteen-pounder gun, let alone a machine-gun.

We'd been inside the street-fighting area's buildings, while grenade-throwing and machine-gunning were actually going on. We'd gone in there looking for dud and spent cartridges. It's amazing we weren't blown up – it's amazing I'm talking to you now. We were on the aircraft-strafing ranges too, when aircraft were practising . . .

Security? *What* security? We sat and played inside the cockpits of the airplanes on the aerodrome.

We watched the Marines – they had Dinky Toys – *our* Dinky Toys by rights – for planning their war-games. Hornby Trains too – that should have come to us. They'd taken *our* toys – why shouldn't we take theirs?

We'd walked off the rifle-range with a Bren-gun before then. We had it hidden. The officer cadets had been firing it, but they went off for a brew-up in their billy-cans and left it. Then we saw the cadet who'd left it getting into trouble, so we went and told the sergeant where we'd put it. It was only a joke, like, a bit of a prank.

We had a grenade, and took the pin out. It went off and singed us pretty badly. Luckily the explosion went the other way, and blew our fireplace in.

We'd had our eye on those 0.22 rifles for quite a while. There were guns lying about everywhere. What else was there for us to do? We saw it as a challenge, I suppose ...

We knew where the guns were – we'd been watching that armoury for ages – it was only an ordinary house in the village street. We knew they always left the window open in hot weather. The armoury was well guarded – but we waited till the guard was being changed and they were all out on parade out front. (We knew their every move.) Then we nipped in the window and got the rifles and ammo. *They reckoned we took 400 rounds of ammo, but it was 5,000 rounds. The authorities were trying to play it down because they were embarrassed about their lack of security, I suppose.*

We fired and fired for hours on end, but we never hurt anybody. It was the poultry-keeper who started off the alarm.

We had about 2,000 soldiers out looking for us, for 38 hours – officer cadets, Marines, police, fire brigade, the lot. *The Marines didn't know who they were looking for, because our cover was so good. From the hills we had a view right over the town and we could see them coming for miles. We even strolled back to the beach and watched them combing the hills for us. What a laugh!* [At this point, other army units were telegraphing the Marines, offering help.] *They fired off blank cartridges to try to scare us out into the open. When they caught us, they gave us a whole Swiss Roll each to eat.*

They marched us through Barmouth with fixed bayonets – we were led by four armed captains, and surrounded by three more, and all the troops marching behind. I don't know why they were allowed to march with fixed bayonets – surely soldiers can only do that if their regiment's been given the Freedom of Barmouth?

My employer threw rotten tomatoes at the soldiers escorting us.

We were locked up for a week in an approved school.

[The lads paid for their prank with an appearance at Barmouth Juvenile Court.]

They marched us into court, and sitting up with the Judges were officers in red hats – brigadiers, field-marshals, I don't know. The court was surrounded by troops with fixed bayonets. I suppose they were making a show – the brass hats were upset.

It was all a childish escapade, but boys will be boys.

Towards the end of that account, I have included comments made by the other boys to David Jack of the *Sunday People*. This is to give the story unity, but the comments by the other boys are in italics. The boys remain nameless, for that is their wish. They have since lived law-abiding respectable lives and deserve their privacy. Their doings and identity since 1944 are of no interest to this book.

But there are many questions unanswered about the Battle of Barmouth. Were the hidden rifles never found; are they still cached in some cave on Cader Idris? What was the feeling in the town; did anyone but one employer throw rotten tomatoes at the soldiers? Was there a lot of feeling – *nationalist* feeling? Why the display of armed might? How upset *were* the top brass? Or was this merely an example of that ancient tribal way in which adolescent boys *will* imitate the habits of their masculine elders? Was Barmouth a military pressure-cooker that boiled them into one wild mad escapade? Perhaps we will never know. Their contemporaries regarded them as heroes. What did their parents think?

8th June, 1946

To-DAY, AS WE CELEBRATE VICTORY, I send this personal message to you and all other boys and girls at school. For you have shared in the hardships and dangers of a total war and you have shared no less in the triumph of the Allied Nations.

I know you will always feel proud to belong to a country which was capable of such supreme effort; proud, too, of parents and elder brothers and sisters who by their courage, endurance and enterprise brought victory. May these qualities be yours as you grow up and join in the common effort to establish among the nations of the world unity and peace.

George R.I.

Acknowledgements

Photographs:

Auckland Collection: 77; BBC Copyright Photograph: 34; BBC Hulton Picture Library: 40, 43, 46, 75, 105 (below), 108, 111 (above), 118, 151, 184 (above), 192 (above); The Bodleian Library, John Johnson Collection: 20; The British Library: 185 (above) © D.C. Thompson and Co. Ltd. Reprinted, by permission, from the *Dandy* 6 January 1940; Tom Cherry: 235; Colorific!: 227; Express Newspapers: 76, 79; Imperial War Museum: 49 (above), 86, 89, 93 (above), 94, 96, 105 (above), 106, 116, 155 (left), 156 (above and below), 157, 160, 166–9, 175, 180, 186; Institute of Agricultural History and Museum of English Rural Life, Reading: 53, 202, 208; Liverpool Daily Post & Echo: 136; Photo Source: 33, 35, 39, 42, 45, 47, 49 (below), 59, 72, 80, 82, 93 (below), 112, 139, 145, 148, 152, 153, 155 (right), 158, 183, 187; Popperfoto: 117, 119 (above), 172–3, 188; George Rodger, Magnum Photos: 17, 114; Courtesy of Roedean School: 165; Syndication International: 63, 83, 90, 100, 119 (below), 131, 192 (below), 196, 212–13; John Topham Picture Library: 14, 23, 24, 26, 27, 30 (above and below), 50, 56, 84, 97, 111 (below), 124, 154, 177, 179, 182, 184 (above and below), 185 (below), 190, 199, 216, 222, 225.

The map on page 61 was redrawn by Raymond Turvey.

Picture research by Susan Rose-Smith and Patience Trevor.

Grateful acknowledgement is made to the following for permission to reprint previously published or broadcast material:

The British Broadcasting Corporation: two excerpts from 1939 BBC radio broadcasts.

Collins Publishers: two excerpts from *Living Through the Blitz* by Tom Harrison (Collins, 1976).

Granada Publishing Limited and David Higham Associates Limited: Excerpt from *The World is a Wedding* by Bernard Kops. (McGibbon and Kee, 1963, now published by Vallentine Mitchell).

Her Majesty the Queen: memories of V.E. Day given to Godfrey Talbot, broadcast in *The Way We Were* on BBC Radio 4, 8 May 1985.

Norman Longmate: excerpt from *How We Lived Then* by Norman Longmate (Hutchinson, 1971).

Macdonald and Charles Scribner's Sons: excerpt from *The Hardest Day* by Alfred Price, copyright © 1979 Alfred Price.

Marshall Cavendish: excerpt from *The War Papers* (no. 27).